Valentino
ROSSI

Dedication

For Bill Brightman
One of Valentino's biggest, littlest fans

Acknowledgements

Big thanks to Valentino and everyone else who helped with this book. All these and more: Aprilia, Luigino 'Gibo' Badioli, Max Biaggi, Rossano Brazzi, Jerry Burgess, Barry Coleman, Mick Doohan, Carlo Fiorani, Rossana Fuzzi, Gold and Goose, Mark Graham, Ross Holleron, Honda Racing Corporation, Hamish Jamieson, Eva Jirsenska, Henk Keulemans, Mac Mackay, Niall Mackenzie, Elena Manzoni, Charlotte Menard, *Motosprint*, Elena Radina, Dr Martin Raines, Wayne Rainey, Kenny Roberts, Graziano Rossi, Stefania Rossi, Giampiero Sacchi, Stefano Saragoni, Kevin Schwantz, Michael Scott, Gigi Soldano, Koji Sugita, Hidenobu Takeuchi, Chris Walker, Warren Willing and Debbie van Zon.

Another title by Mat Oxley

Mick **Doohan**
Thunder from Down Under by Mat Oxley. Second edition

First published in 2002

A catalogue record for this book is available from the British Library

ISBN 1 85960 891 4

Library of Congress catalog card no. 2002104054

Published by Haynes Publishing, Sparkford, Yeovil, Somerset, BA22 7JJ, UK

Tel: 01963 442030 Fax: 01963 440001
Int. tel: +44 1963 442030 Int. fax: +44 1963 440001
E-mail: sales@haynes-manuals.co.uk
Website: www.haynes.co.uk

Haynes North America, Inc.,
861 Lawrence Drive, Newbury Park,
California 91320, USA

Printed and bound in England by
J. H. Haynes & Co. Ltd, Sparkford

Opposite: A hair colour too far at Donington '99. It didn't last long, the hair clippers were out a few days later. (Milagro)

Valentino
ROSSI

MotoGenius *by Mat Oxley*

Contents

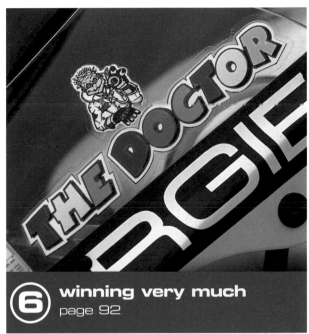

by Mick Doohan
foreword
500 World Champion 1994-1998

Valentino continues to surprise me. More than anything, it's his mental strength. He's got the capability to stay right on it week after week, which is where the other guys fall short. For sure he's fast, but some of the others are fast too. It's his mental strength that pulls him through. If ever he has a problem and a little doubt creeps in, he pulls through and he's stronger than before.

Ever since he's been in GPs he's been good for the sport. He's a colourful character, he loves life, he loves riding motorcycles and he wants to portray that to everybody. He arrived and changed the way people think about racing. He proved that you can have fun, even though he's very serious and focused.

Also, he's a team player. He doesn't believe he's the only guy in the team and that's really important in racing. Sure, he's lucky to have Jerry Burgess and the team working with him, like I was – because JB's got so much experience – but he has got a very good feeling for the motorcycle. He understands what's going on around him, which is why he tends to stay on. A lot of guys feel what's going on but they don't know how to translate the feeling to their engineers.

Valentino is at a point in his career where the pressure could get to him, but even during 2001 when the pressure was really there, he was on top of it, he didn't let it distract him, so I don't think that's going to be a problem. The biggest factor in his future is going to be how long he wants to continue riding and this is an issue that Valentino alone will determine.

I've known author Mat Oxley even longer than I've known Valentino, since I first came to GPs in '89. That season was a bit of a struggle for me, but Mat was one guy who kept writing that I might have some ability long-term. Since then he's become one of the most respected media guys in the paddock. He tells things like they are; he's a straight-shooter. He'll give praise when it's deserved and criticise when it's warranted. As a rider, you can't ask for more than that.

Mick Doohan
Gold Coast, Australia, May 2002

Mick Doohan,
2000 Portuguese
GP. (Gold & Goose)

introduction

Motorcycle racing is a funny old game. In fact it is *the* funny old game of 'I can go faster than you' amplified to the nth degree; grown men risking life and limb for ego.

This book is about a man who has played this game like few others, achieving an extraordinary run of successes while wearing a smile as wide as his extravagant racing lines. Valentino Rossi just loves racing motorcycles, and his infectious enthusiasm for speed and two wheels has transported him into the mainstream and helped change the way the world looks at bike racing. As someone recently said, Rossi is not your 'typical motorcycle racing psychopath'.

Valentino skipped into the World Championship arena seven years ago as a mopheaded teenager. 'Who's that girl?' people asked. Now, as a bewhiskered London geezer, his face is more recognised than any motorcyclist's in history. Rossi has become GP racing, he's a phenomenon, and yet he's a rider on a multi-million pound salary who still likes to muck about with the stickers on his race bike. That's not normal.

Valentino keeps it simple, stays true to his roots. He's a rider who thinks deeply about his racing but never out-thinks himself. His philosophy is straightforward: think hard, have fun. He isn't a desperate trier, he's a natural, doing the right thing comes easily to him, whether it's riding right or looking right. The man understands.

He approaches his racing both as boy and man, both as art and science. To him the art of the racing line is 'like a poem', which is why he can magic the kind of lines of which most racers seem incapable. As paddock philosopher Dr Claudio Costa says: 'Valentino abandons himself to the creativity of the mind so that he can play the game of life according to the carefree rules of the child.'

And yet he is almost digitally efficient. 'The weirdest thing that happens to me when I'm racing,' he says, 'is that I perceive the race not as a unit but as a succession of fragments that pass before my eyes in slow motion.' Which may go some way to explaining how he unerringly applied his relentless two-year programme to deal with the 125, 250 and 500 World Championships; one year to explore each new class, one year to conquer. But this season he has ditched the two-year plan, dominating the new four-stroke MotoGP class from the outset. His touch, it seems, is more golden than that of King Midas.

Valentino is so good at racing, so good at life, that he seems almost too good to be true, like the invention of some Hollywood scriptwriter with a Superman complex who writes an impossible amount of genius and nobility into his male lead. Of course, Rossi isn't Superman, he just likes to dress that way sometimes…

Mat Oxley
London, England, May 2002

Valentino has done a bit of growing up over the past few years, revealing a more contemplative side. (Gold & Goose)

il fenomeno ROSSI

Rossi mania grabbed me for the first time during the 1979 British GP at Silverstone. Standing at Stowe Corner amongst the crumpled beer cans, I watched Graziano Rossi lay waste to the 250 pack, his extravagant style and the speed of his lovely Morbidelli moving him well clear of that year's world champ, Kawasaki's Kork Ballington. With just three corners to go he had stretched his advantage to an unbeatable 2.5 seconds. Then he crashed.

As a reckless 20-year-old I thought that was pretty cool – chucking away a surefire win like he just didn't care. Why slow down just because you can almost taste the champagne? Rossi was a motorcycle racer doing what he thought he was paid to do: going as fast as he possibly could, from green light to chequered flag. Silverstone should've been his fourth win of the

year, instead it was the last time he got close to winning a grand prix.

Papa Rossi also looked pretty damn fly, like Jesus, only much faster. His leathers and helmet were white, rent through by a zigzag lightning streak of red and green for the Italian tricolor, and his shoulder-length hair whipped around from beneath his helmet. But it wasn't a dodgy haircut, Rossi was way too cool, way too charismatic, to ever look wrong. In fact, he was so right that I used to spend evenings doing sketches of my own Rossi-replica leathers and helmet, which I kind of knew I'd never get around to owning.

Rossi retired a few years later, a nasty bump on the head forcing an end to a career that never made the most of his intelligence and riding talent. He faded from my memory after I started racing, still without

A phenomenon on the bike and never anything less than mighty cool off it: That's your Valentino. (Milagro)

those red, white and green leathers. Twelve years later I spotted him off a bike for the first time, not counting that moment he'd parted company with his Morbidelli at Silverstone. During the summer of '91 I was in the Adriatic resort of Rimini doing a story on Italy's latest craze, minimoto racing, and there he was, stood by the track beneath the floodlights (it was almost midnight), watching intently. I went over to shake his hand, to tell him he'd been a hero of mine and to ask him what he was doing at some dodgy minimoto track in the middle of the night. Rossi pointed into the gloom, at a midget figure circulating the midget racetrack on a midget bike. 'Is my son, Valentino,' he grinned. 'Good to meet you,' I replied, and not wanting to cause any further embarrassment to either of us, I made my excuses and left papa and bambino to themselves, never thinking I'd see them again.

Of course, I got to see plenty of them, we all did. Over the next decade the little kid would grow into a big kid, dazzling pretty much the whole world with his speed and charisma, his ever so slightly eccentric dad along for the ride, eschewing flash hotels to sleep in the back of his BMW.

It wouldn't be too much of an exaggeration to say that Valentino Rossi has changed the face of grand prix racing; certainly no other bike racer has ever got closer to being a pop star. And his actual racing achievements are awe-inspiring, history-making stuff: first GP win at the age of 17, first world title at 18, another title at 20,

his first 500 win a few months after his 21st birthday, and the 500 World Championship a year later. He's the fourth youngest rider to have worn the 500 crown, the youngest man to have won three world titles and at the age of just 23 he's already well into the top ten all-time GP winners' list.

His progress has been so relentless that it smacks of the automaton sportsman – grim-faced, head down, no thought for anything but total victory – and yet each and every one of his successes has been achieved with a joy that never fails to touch everyone's heart. 'Valentino likes to win, he's a great fighter,' says his engineer Jerry Burgess, who's worked closely with the youngster since the end of 1999. 'But he also knows we're in the entertainment business, so he likes to entertain.'

Even back in his 125 and 250 days his infectious enthusiasm was breaking the sport to whole new audiences, amongst them the Valenteenyboppers, gangs of Italian schoolgirls drawn to racetracks by their heart-throb's pretty blue eyes. Valentino doesn't appreciate that kind of attention though because he's a bit of a biking purist. 'They're not fans of Rossi the motorcycle racer, but just because I've got blue eyes, I don't like,' he says with faint exasperation after years spent fleeing these seething ranks of moist, pubescent Latin lovelies. 'It's good to have one or two nice girls chasing you, but not one thousand.' That's what he says, but you wonder if he really means it once you've been

Graziano's influence on his son has been immeasurable, all the way from riding bicycles... (Rossi family archive)

Giving full
backing at the
crucial first
minimoto races
which helped
Valentino build
the foundations
of his talent.
(Rossi family
archive)

Vale's baptism
into the world of
GP racing and
dad's still there.
(Henk Keulemans)

inside his motorhome, watching him and constant companion Uccio Salucci giggling madly as they field lewd text messages from female admirers.

For all his talent and his charm Rossi is a sponsors' darling, and yet he stays true to himself, tells it like it is, he doesn't do PR spew. Like he's never afraid to voice his dislike of bitter-rival Max Biaggi and that's something in GP racing, where everyone has got into the habit of 'sugaring each others' asses', as former 500 champ King Kenny Roberts once put it.

Valentino knows how to make people laugh too. Perhaps his cheesiest post-race celebrations have been a mite overdone but he was pure comedy at Jerez '99, dumping his Aprilia RSW250 halfway around the victory lap and diving into a marshals' trackside Portaloo, emerging seconds later to 150,000 fans going off their nuts.

So what has he got that other racers haven't? He's a phenomenon, the leader of a new breed of cool GP racer, a bright, enlightened 21st century version of the macho hell-raisers of old. Maybe there's never been a rider who combines such warmth of character with so much natural talent, raw bravery and tireless dedication.

To dissect and understand the Rossi phenomenon we should begin by looking further back than his immediate genes. We must look to where he comes from, because his national culture is just as important as his inherited family characteristics. Italy is the heart and soul of motorsport, Italians are obsessed with speed, and when it comes to racing as romance, they're the kings, from Ducati to Ferrari, from Agostini to Nuvolari, from Monza to the Mille Miglia.

Italy's record of bike racing glory is beyond compare. During 53 years of motorcycle grand prix racing, Italian riders have scored almost twice as many 125, 250 and 500 grand prix victories as any other nation. By the end of the 2001 season, Italians had won 491 GPs, the British are next with 276 victories, then the Americans (169), the Japanese (149) and the Spanish (139).

Valentino is just the latest in a long lineage of

racetrack conquerors that goes way back to the pre-war exploits of Tazio Nuvolari (the grand prix car legend who started out on bikes) and thence to 1950 500 World Champion Umberto Maseti, Sixties' and Seventies' heroes Giacomo Agostini, Walter Villa and Renzo Pasolini, Eighties' 500 World Champions Marco Lucchinelli and Franco Uncini, and current names like Biaggi, Loris Capirossi and Manuel Poggiali.

So from where do the Italians get their lust for speed, what are its roots? Their passion goes back to the start of the 20th century, to the earliest days of the motor industry when Italy fell head over heels in love with the machine and the future that machines might offer. Futurism was an Italian cultural phenomenon, fuelled by the birth of the new technological society, a new age of noise and speed: aeroplanes, cars, motorcycles and telecommunications. 'We declare that the world's splendour has been enriched by a new beauty: the beauty of speed,' proclaimed Italy's 1909 manifesto of Futurism. 'A racing motor car, its frame adorned

with great pipes, like snakes with explosive breath…a roaring motor car, which seems to run on shrapnel…' Okay, so they were getting a bit carried away but you can see what they meant, and it's no different now; in Britain people hate noisy cars and bikes, in Italy they love 'em.

Officially sanctioned long-distance street races, roaring from one town to the next, exploded across Italy during the 1920s as the nation's big five motorcycle factories (the so-called Pentarchia of Benelli, Bianchi, Garelli, Gilera and Guzzi) fought for supremacy in the showrooms by fighting for supremacy on the 'racetracks'. Such was the national passion for these often lethal events that Italy was the last Continental nation to ban racing on public roads. Italy's powered two-wheeler industry really took off after the Second World War when the rapidly industrialising nation needed to get the largely peasant workforce out of the villages and into the factories. The workers required transport but cars were beyond their meagre wages, so the scooter was born. Lambretta and Vespa were both established in 1946, and four years later Ducati and Aermacchi joined the race for mobilisation.

As sales boomed, so did the race scene. Most of the manufacturers were enthusiastic in their involvement and naturally signed local riders who could communicate with their engineers and promote sales in the all-important home market, as Biaggi and Rossi did so well for Aprilia half a century later. (It is no coincidence that the vast majority of Britain's 276 GP successes were achieved when the country had a motorcycle industry.)

It is more difficult to ponder exactly when the Italians first fell in love with engineering and maybe it would be pushing the point to speculate that the first sparks were ignited by Leonardo da Vinci and the Renaissance way back in the 15th and 16th centuries. Or maybe not, for Italy has been renowned for its artisans ever since. The metal workers who toiled at Enzo Ferrari's first workshops, for example, were craftsmen continuing Modena's centuries-old reputation for skilled manufacture of just about anything in metal. Of course, there are other less complex reasons for Italy's ongoing motorcycling success story, like the fact that the sun shines a whole lot more down there than it does in northern Europe.

Whatever, Valentino's Italian blood is a major factor in his success, in all kinds of ways. He has that Latin lust for life and a sunny, catholic attitude, he's enthusiastic,

Can't live with 'em; can't live without 'em. Rossi has attracted a whole new breed of fan to GPs, even if he doesn't have a big love for the Valenteenyboppers. (Milagro)

There's no escape, especially in Japan everyone wants a slice of Valentino. (Mark Wernham)

He's always been a team player, inspiring and delighting the people around him. This is his 125 title-winning crew in 1997. (Milagro)

loquacious and determined to have fun, even though he's involved in a deadly serious business. His attitude to life and to racing demands inevitable comparisons with that of Mick Doohan, the man who dominated 500 GPs when Valentino was riding 125s and 250s, and whose team he inherited after the Australian quit racing at the end of 1999.

In fact, 'The Doctor' and 'Mighty Mick' have little in common, apart from their blinding talent to ride a motorcycle faster than anyone else on this planet. Doohan was a driven man, to the scariest of degrees, he used to go racing like there were demons chasing him, and if he ever slowed down, they'd have him. There was a terrorised urgency to his riding, he forced the bike down into corners, hunched over the front like some kind of desperado; 'all prick and ribs like a drover's dog', as the Aussies would say. Who knows what drove him, but the inside of a racer's head is a strange place: weird forces driving weird psyches to take weird risks, and maybe the pain that cut right through his injury-blighted career coloured his temperament. Valentino (so far, touch wood, relatively unscarred by racing) doesn't seem to possess that kind of mildly psychotic inner self and really does look like he's having fun on the bike; he looks more natural, more fluid, more smooth. Off track he appears remarkably well adjusted, with few obvious signs of that often ruinous desperation to prove himself bigger and braver than everyone else, which is the defining behavioural characteristic of so many racers. Mostly he just seems to be having a ball.

'I've always said Mick enjoyed winning and Valentino enjoys racing,' adds Burgess, who previously guided Doohan to his five 500 crowns. 'If Valentino has a great race and finishes second, he's disappointed but he's not angry with the world like Mick used to be, he's not going to tear your head off.'

Former journalist Barry Coleman, who covered the World Championships when Rossi senior was racing, knows from where he got those characteristics. 'Graziano was anything but a typical motorcycle racing psychopath,' Coleman recalls. 'He's a marvellous man and it's inevitable that Valentino has taken a lot from having a dad like that. Valentino recently said: "I'm just a fan on a bike", and I think that's exactly how he is.'

Too true, Vale (as mates call him, pronounced 'Valay') was a dedicated GP anorak long before he started racing, with an encyclopaedic knowledge of riders' helmet designs, numbers and liveries. One of his earliest visits to a GP is burned into his memory, as it would be in the mind of any ordinary race fan. 'The first GP I remember going to see was Mugello '91,' he says. 'I used to watch all the races on TV, so I knew all the riders' numbers, all their helmet designs, the whole circus. I was with Gibo (Badioli, old family friend and now his manager) and Graziano. We parked the camper at Casanova Savelli (a daunting, downhill right–left flick where his fan club now camps out) and I remember very well the 125 race with Ueda, with number 56 and the green and blue Hero Sports Honda, fighting with Capirossi and Gresini.' This is not normal. Most riders hold zero interest in other racers, except their direct competitors, but Valentino really is an enthusiast. He can even recognise a journalist's helmet design. When I was researching this book he grabbed my lid and said: 'Yes, I remember your helmet from when I was a boy reading *Motosprint* [Italy's biking weekly], didn't you have a big accident one day, going under a truck?' Well, yes, I did. So what can we tell from this? That he's bright, that he's got a good memory, but most of all that he's interested in ordinary people, which is a serious rarity in the me-me-me world of GP racing. Some top-line racers show less interest in people like us than some folk might in their dustman.

He is even aware that it's pretty weird having his biography published when he's only 23 (in fact this is the fourth Rossi book in as many summers). 'Yes,' he grins. 'Is strange, but I don't take it serious, it's not possible to take everything serious, in life or in racing. If possible I take it with a smile, it makes life easier.'

Valentino's uncomplicated, unaffected, unpretentious attitude to life and racing is everything. Nowadays, GPs are more intense, if less lethal, than they've ever been. Track safety may be better than ever but the danger is still there, and grand prix riders tend to crash more often these days, because the demands and rewards of World Championship racing drive them to exist on the outer extremes of traction. Some crashes hurt more than others; very few don't hurt at

Visor down, head down, Valentino walks to work, ready to shut out the madness that fills his off-track life. (Gold & Goose)

all. Highsides (racing's equivalent of flinging yourself out of a speeding express train) hardly ever happen without a subsequent visit to Dr Claudio Costa's Clinica Mobile for a dose of mesotherapy, a local pain-relief therapy that can require more than 100 micro-injections. As Valentino says: 'I have very much fear of the mesotherapy needle. Of course, I'm scared about getting hurt, but what am I going to do, lock myself in a room and be happy being safe?'

The further psychological pressures on top riders are crushing, impossible to overestimate, and come from every direction – from the factory, from the sponsors, from the team, from the media, from the fans and, of course, from inside the rider himself. Sure, there's harder ways to make a living, but when these guys aren't on the bike they're huddled for hours in debriefing sessions with their engine, chassis and tyre engineers, surrounded by the flicker of computer monitors and the whirr-whirr of hard drives. And if they're not doing that, they're being gushed over by their sponsors, suffocated by the fans or harangued by the media. Racing becomes a chore.

Which is why so many modern-day riders are anything but a bundle of laughs. In TV interviews they stare at the camera, mouthing weary platitudes because their minds are burdened by some hi-tech conundrum: transient engine behaviour, high-speed rebound damping curves and data-logging outputs. Valentino seems to be one of the few top guys who

has this sorted. By keeping the joy, he rides at his very best. He rides fast because he wants to, because it's a blast. Many of his rivals have let the serious stuff get to them, so they've stopped having fun, so they struggle to be as quick, week in, week out.

Back in bike racing's so-called golden days – the Fifties, Sixties and Seventies – GP racers were fast-living, up-for-a-laugh daredevils, apparently able to win races with inspired, risk-taking heroics. Back then racing was an art and racers behaved accordingly: out on the piss, sniffing and snorting their way through ranks of glamorous shags.

It's not like that anymore. Racing at grand prix level is now a science and racers are the front-line laboratory troops, they just wear leathers instead of white lab coats. It's not only about white-knuckle, devil-may-care risk taking anymore, nowadays racing is a cold and precise science – a giant, globally televised physics experiment. Sure, racers need balls just as much as they ever did, but only as much as they need to understand the science of it all. Sixties' legend Mike Hailwood, who like Valentino won his first 500 crown at the age of 22, was happily technophobic. Vale may not be a rocket scientist but he needs to be able to discuss deep technical concepts with his crew for hours and hours. As King Kenny Roberts puts it: 'People say the riders aren't the same fun guys they used to be, well, they don't have the time to be, that's the whole thing.'

There is a parallel here with the USAF's jet-fighter

This ancient ritual stretches his leathers and legs, and leaves the pedestrian world behind, and focuses his mind on the track. (Gold & Goose)

Vale and 250
chief Brazzi get to
know one another
in 1998. 'The
hard thing was
leaving his team;
they'd become like
family.' (Milagro)

test pilots, as described in Hunter S. Thompson's book *The Great Shark Hunt*. The gun-totin' acid casualty author talks of how, during the Sixties, the USAF developed 'a computerised version of the legendary, hell-for-leather test pilot', banishing the old 'kick the tyre, light the fire and away we go' heroes of old. He goes on: 'the best pilot in the world – even if he could land a B-52 on the number eight green at Pebble Beach without taking a divot – would be useless on a test-flight project unless he could explain, in a written report, just how and why the landing could be made.'

It's the same with modern racers – GP bikes are so hi-tech that riders must be able to describe machine behaviour in acute detail, then analyse potential improvements with their technicians. And there's another link between old fliers and GP racers. Thompson describes how USAF test pilots used to get their off-duty kicks on terra firma around their base in the Mojave desert: 'back in the good old days, when men were men and might was right and the devil took the hindmost, the peaceful desert highways were raceways for off-duty pilots on big motorcycles. Slow-moving travellers were frequently blown off the road by wildmen in leather jackets and white scarves, human torpedoes defying all

speed limits and heedless of their own safety.'

Not any more, when he revisited the base years later Thompson found the USAF appalled at the idea of anything as fun and as dangerous as a motorcycle. 'Today's pilots go to bed early, and regard big motorcycles with the same analytical disdain they have for hippies, winos and other failure symbols. They take their risks, on assignment, between dawn and 4.30pm'. In GP racing, it's Sundays between noon and 3pm.

That's exactly what Valentino found when he came to GPs in 1996. If Doohan had raised dedication and commitment to a new level, the Australian's psychotic approach to racing had transformed paddock atmosphere. Mighty Mick was breaking everyone's balls (including his own), he brought withering aggression and unrelenting pressure to his racing, because that's what he needed to win. And he was so successful that everyone mimicked his attitude until the paddock became almost unbearably intense. Valentino wanted to change all that, he couldn't imagine going racing and not having fun, he'd hate it, what'd be the point? So he changed things.

'When I came to GPs all the riders were very, very serious,' he recalls. 'So when I started winning, me and my friends decided we should try to make some big fun. We just wanted to do something new to show the big emotion of winning races. The ideas usually came to us in a bar in Tavullia at two in the morning! They were just a game, just some fun with my fan club.'

From the Portaloo gag to the prank with the blow-up doll, through his entire alter ego wardrobe from Robin Hood to Superman, and through his numerous Madonna-like makeovers from girly mophead to bearded ragamuffin via skinhead and trance cadet, Valentino tells the world that he likes a laugh. It's all just good fun, though there's little doubt there's an element of palliative here, as if to ward off the round-the-clock stress that gets to many big-time riders. By halfway through a GP season some riders look burned out and ground down, but Valentino counteracts the pressure, even though, or perhaps because, he's the most sought after of all, his every step dogged by a ravenous pack of Italian media, shades on, notebooks in hand, pretending to be his mate.

No motorcycle racer has ever been bigger than Rossi, not even glam Seventies' superstar Barry Sheene who was famously namechecked in a top-ten hit. He is, if you like, the David Beckham of bikes and, like Becks, he pays a high price for his fame having crossed over into the mainstream. Like Becks and Andre Agassi, he's the guy who transcended his sport's own territory, because he doesn't only appeal to blokes. The ladies, the Valenteenies and the kids love him too; so these days whole families sit down to watch GP racing like never before.

Valentino arrived at the pinnacle of his sport with impeccable timing, for motorcycle racing needed someone with mainstream pulling power if it was to thrust itself into the global consciousness. Like any other 21st century sport, bike racing is a commodity that has to be sold to as many consumers as possible, and Valentino's sweet, smiling face is exactly what the sport, and the corporations behind it, were looking for, the weapon that would fire their products deep into the wish lists of consumers. Indeed, there've been times over the last few years when it appears that Rossi is grand prix racing, he is its sun, the rest of the show just orbits around him.

'Jeez, isn't he great?' Valentino's HRC squad (from left: Bernard Ansiau, Alex Briggs, Jerry Burgess, Dick Smart and Gary Coleman) can hardly believe how easy he is to work with, even when asked to oblige for dudgy 'Doctor' photo shoots. (Henk Keulemans)

As a result, his life is barely his own these days, indeed he is so popular at home that he's had to exile himself to London. The pressures of celebrity really began to bite home as he strode towards the 500 title in 2001. Battered by the incessant demands of the media, his sweet nature hardened somewhat, the perma-grin of his 125 and 250 years buckled; it had to if he was to preserve his sanity. And he gave up his more outlandish post-race celebrations. This, after all, is what we do to the celebrities we adore. We squeeze out of them exactly what it is that we love within them, as Oscar Wilde once observed, we kill the things we love.

Even so, Valentino is still as at ease with his mind-boggling fame as it's possible to be. And in that sense he's the very opposite of his predecessor Doohan, who couldn't help but look agonisingly, but endearingly, awkward whenever thrust into the limelight outside of his helmet. Doohan, you see, never crossed into the mainstream, never ever wanted to. Roberts again: 'The things that make Valentino popular are also the things that make life hard for him. If you're only a good motor-cycle racer it's one thing, but the more your face gets splashed around the place for selling sunglasses, watches and stuff like that, the more problems you're going to have. For every plus there's a minus, and the more pluses, the more minuses. That's the way the world works, we didn't invent it, we just have to live in it.'

The devastating demands of riding the fastest bikes on earth have also made their mark. Like Doohan, Eighties' 500 king Eddie Lawson and many others before him, Valentino's face has aged rapidly since he moved on from 250s: the cheeks more hollow, the eyes more sunken, the look a little more haunted. That's what 200 horsepower motorcycles do to you.

And yet despite the pressurised lifestyle, both on an off the track, he obviously does love what he's doing, and like Becks, he's fully aware of the Faustian contract he's made with fame. 'For sure there is more good than bad to being famous,' says Rossi with a glint in his eye. 'The bad thing is the stress. Now I can't go anywhere in the world without being recognised. Very many people recognise me and want autographs and photos. The

situation is a little better in London but Italy is a nightmare, a nightmare, I will never be able to live a normal life there. Fame affects you in different ways; when you have many fans who follow you like a slipstream, yes, it's heavy, but it's good. But the Italian journalists only follow me for one reason, they're waiting for a mistake. If I say one word wrong or if I crash, it's 'Ah, fack, he's stupid!'. Fack? Yes, fack. Since he moved to London Vale has revealed a growing love for the 'F' word, delivered with an Italian intonation, like 'sack!'. The word obviously doesn't hold the same sting for him that it does for some Anglo-Saxons; presumably it's the Latin derivative of the Gaelic 'Feck'…

Amidst the madness Valentino keeps it real by surrounding himself with mates, most of whom he's known since they got together to make some mischief in primary school. He doesn't do the celebrity circuit. His thick-as-thieves Latin homies call themselves the Tavullia Chihuahua (Tavullia, his hometown in Italy, the Chihuahua, a tribe of North American Indians), although, of course, this is only the inner sanctum;

Happy Vale. A real Italian is never far from a bar and an espresso machine. (Milagro)

Aprilia weren't slow to use Valentino's star quality to flog scooters. 'I'd do anything for my SR,' says this 1998 ad. (Aprilia)

when Vale wrapped up the 500 title in Australia , more than 2000 Tavullians stayed up partying until 6am, watching the race on a big screen in the town piazza. No wonder he cherishes the anonymity of London.

Former 500 champion Kevin Schwantz, whom many older fans see as a kind of proto-Rossi because he shares a similar attitude to life and racing, remembers the stresses of racing being one of the hardest things to handle during his years at the top. 'I always found there was so much pressure, and a lot of it self-inflicted,' says the '93 champ. 'You put so much pressure on yourself to be the best that you've got to keep telling yourself that it's fun, because if it ever quits being fun it's really not worth it, because however much you're making, there's a lot on the line, you could get hurt in nothing flat. When I wasn't liking it anymore, I decided to stop. The thing with Rossi is that he's having fun, so he's out on the track every time wringing the bike's neck, trying to get everything he can out of it.'

Fellow American Roberts, who went on to become a successful team owner after winning his three 500

titles, agrees with Schwantz. 'I think Rossi's secret is pretty simple,' he says. 'It looks to me like he's loving it, he's happy to be out there. He doesn't play mind games, he loves riding the motorcycle, and he rides it right. That's a hard combination to beat; then when you get the best rider on the best bike, that's a hard combination to beat, too. If he keeps going like this, he'll set a lot of records and be one of the best, for sure. He's is definitely up there, but only time will tell if he's the greatest ever. The only thing that could happen is that he'll get burned out, but I don't see that, he's having more fun than anyone.'

And yet, is this impression of a straightforward young man having a ball the real Valentino? Maybe not entirely, believes Giampiero Sacchi, the urbane Italian manager who brought the mop-haired 16-year-old into GP racing back in 1996. 'The Valentino concept is this,' says Sacchi. 'He wants other people to think that he's just having fun but for sure he's not just having fun, inside he's saying: 'You think I'm just crazy but I'm not'. I think this is the key to understanding Valentino; you watch him and it looks like he's just having fun, but if you watch him more carefully you realise there's nothing casual about what he does, everything happens for a reason, his is a very studied performance, he's thinking about all the details, all the time.' In other words, there's a fair dose of cunning in his make-up. Of course there is, no guileless rider ever won a world championship.

No wimp ever won a World Championship either,

so how come someone so apparently sweet-natured as Valentino has carved such a swathe through the sport? Bike racing is a vicious game, and while he isn't the kind of rider who strikes fear into rivals by riding out of control, there's no doubt that he takes no shit from anyone when he's on the racetrack. Scary aggression, intimidation and a bit of argy-bargy are all part of racing. 'GP riders don't mind riding into each other,' says Jeremy McWilliams, a stubborn rival during Valentino's ride to his first 500 win at the 2000 British GP. 'You want to pass as cleanly as possible, but if you're getting frustrated and it's the last lap, you ride into the guy. And it helps if you've got a bit of a reputation for being crazy. You need to stamp your authority on the other guys when you're making a move.'

People love Valentino because he's capable of racing hard, working hard and enjoying himself. His rivals also work hard but most of them have forgotten how to get their kicks out of what they're doing. Work hard, play hard isn't a new concept but it's a concept lost on many of today's richly rewarded sports stars, whether they're Formula One drivers, tennis players or bike racers. And there's something deeply unattractive about watching someone getting paid serious money for doing what they love and yet remaining so determinedly miserable. Vale could never do that, whatever the hours he puts into his racing. 'And he really does work at it, more than I ever did,' agrees Doohan. 'He's in the garage till all hours of the night, going through

Forced into exile by his fame, Valentino's never too far from an Italian student or two in his adopted home of London. (Milagro)

Valentino and his fans go ape at Jerez '99. However well he takes defeat, he never hides the joy of victory. (Gold & Goose)

stuff with the crew.' Which might go some way to explaining why he's so bad at getting up in the mornings. During his first year in 500s, Valentino badly overslept at the Catalan GP, missing half of morning practice. 'When I wake up I always have a big confusion for the first five minutes,' he says in mitigation. 'Then I remember: "Oh fack, I'm at world grand prix!".'

Few club racers are that laidback and his horizontal demeanour once again contrasts vividly with Doohan, who, you just know, would've been a very different person on race mornings, awakening like some psycho out of a dodgy Hollywood thriller, lying rigid on his back, eyes twitching from tight shut to wild stare in, well, the blink of an eye.

Burgess remembers the Catalunya incident. 'He arrived in the pits in a state of shock, he'd never missed a practice session in his life. When he was at Aprilia his chief mechanic always went down to his motorhome and woke him up, so now it's me that goes and knocks on the door.'

Burgess has always known how to extract the best from his riders. Before Valentino and Doohan, the Aussie helped Freddie Spencer and Wayne Gardner to world titles during the Eighties. He expects 100 per cent commitment both on and off the track, and when he doesn't get it, he tells them exactly what he thinks. Some other crew chiefs won't do that, they're too wary of destabilising their riders. There's no doubt that the Burgess tough love has played its part in Valentino's

recent successes, and yet Burgess is clever enough to realise that his rider wouldn't react well to regimentation. 'Valentino is Valentino, and if you kill that off you may kill off the goose that lays the golden egg,' he says. 'You've got to let him be himself, he certainly doesn't clown around in testing and he's always well applied in practice. In that way he's like Mick, you never see him just riding around, he's on it every lap. He does his own thing after races, but I don't think that affects him, he's just enjoying himself.'

Valentino's character still shines through when he's getting messy at a Sunday night victory party. At Rio 2001, where he wrapped up the last-ever 500 title, he was the star attraction at a Honda celebration party. Sharing a table with mate Marco Melandri, Valentino refused to hog the limelight, instead turning it on Honda's even-younger guns – the Spanish Telefonica Junior team of teen heroes Toni Elias, Daniel Pedrosa and Juan Olive. He invited them to his table to give them a first lesson in heavy drinking, perching uncomfortably on the corner of his chair while Elias enjoyed the comfy part of the seat. That's not normal behaviour for a World Champion – most racers are takers, not givers. They say that nice guys don't win World Championships but Vale does seem to be an exception. He's a giver not a taker, which is why he takes the trouble to entertain his fans. Cynics may say that's all guile to raise his profile, and sure there's guile in there, but most of all it's youthful *joie de vivre*; boys just wanna have fun…

When he's an old man, Rossi will retire to Tavullia and watch the world go by. Part of the town is already a shrine to its home-grown hero. (Milagro)

Honda's 2001 title party in Rio; Valentino gives teen GP stars Toni Elias (left) and Daniel Pedrosa a first lesson in heavy drinking. (Hidenobu Takeuchi)

And Ninja Turtle came too. Vale lays the foundations of his genius at a local minimoto track. (Rossi archive)

making Valentino

Tavullia is your typical sleepy little Italian town, the dusty tranquillity rent asunder by an ancient Vespa struggling up the hill, its gnarled owner hunched over the cockpit, fag hanging from his mouth as he's swamped by a gang of grinning scooter kids, all knees, elbows and dodgy riding styles.

The town is perched on the spur of a hill a few miles inland from the Adriatic and is reached by the kind of twisting country lanes that can give youngsters a taste for speed, the lanes down which cops used to chase Rossi and his gang of grinning scooter kids.

Like most of Italy the place is steeped in history. Tavullia's hillside location made it an important vantage point during the conflicts that raged throughout the peninsula in the centuries that preceded Italian unification in 1871. Strongly socialist for the last century, the region was fiercely anti-fascist during the Mussolini years and a hive of anti-Nazi resistance during the Second World War. German occupation ended in September 1944 after a particularly bloody battle as the Allies pushed their way north through the area's Gothic Line defences.

Almost 60 years after the Germans were defeated Tavullia is firmly in the hands of an army of Valentino Rossi fans. One of the larger buildings in the town's little piazza is painted vivid yellow in celebration of the hometown hero, yellow number 46 flags flutter from house balconies, shop windows are crammed with Rossi posters and locals wander past wearing bright yellow shoes and bright yellow jackets.

Half a mile away, overlooking Tavullia from another hillside, is the house where Valentino grew up

The sparkle in the eyes is already there: on the beach with mum and dad; Winter '81. (Rossi archive)

and rode a motorcycle for the first time. Dad still lives there, with second wife Lorena and their five-year-old daughter Clara. A rusting Lambretta lies on its side in one corner of the garden, but there are few other signs that this is the home of Italy's greatest motorcycling family.

Graziano Rossi wasn't as fast as his son, but he was one of Italy's quickest in the late Seventies and probably would've gone on to win more than just three GPs if his career hadn't been blighted by a couple of serious concussions. You can't know Valentino without knowing his father; meet Graziano and you fully understand why Valentino is the man he is: warmer, smarter and more modest than your average racetrack maniac. Graziano is a bit of a hippy too, a bit of an eccentric, renowned for his wacky helmet designs, extravagant clothing and the apparently bizarre habit of sleeping in the back of his BMW estate when he's at the races. 'I'm really proud to have found the alternative way to live at GPs,' he smiles. 'I don't want to drive a motorhome, I don't want to stay in a hotel because the best time to be with Valentino

is in the evenings, and I can't stay in his motorhome because he never goes to sleep before one. Anyway, I've set up the car nicely, with a mattress like in my own at home. I know people point at me but I don't care, so long as Valentino doesn't say: 'Stop, you're embarrassing me.' You've got to admit it, the guy's got a point.

Papa Rossi was born on 14 March 1954 to a cabinet maker and housewife based in nearby Pesaro, home to the Benelli factory and many Italian racetrack champions. 'Pesaro is Italy's capital of motorcycling,' he reckons. 'All the kids are into bikes, not like the rest of Italy where they're into soccer.' Mama Stefania was born three year later, the daughter of a nurse and a bike-mad truck driver. They were neighbours as kids and got together when they were teenagers, by which time Graziano had already discovered his love of speed while racing his mates on pushbikes. 'We'd have races on the way home from school and I was the fastest downhill,' so it was only a matter of time before he was scraping around for an engine.

'We had no money but my best friend Valentino

was a genius with his hands, he got an engine from here and a chassis from there and built our first motocross bike.' Rossi had wanted to go roadracing but his parents wouldn't sign for his licence, so he started on the dirt. 'For me roadracing was always the dream, it was more colourful, more important and all the real heroes were roadracers, anyone could do motocross.'

The pair worked in seaside restaurants and hotels to scrape together cash for their homebuilt racer until one summer Valentino was drowned in the Adriatic. Graziano still sheds a tear at the memory. 'Many people think we christened Valentino because he was born two days after St Valentine's day, but he's named after my best friend. He'd be Valentino even if he'd been born in December.'

Rossi started roadracing when he was 21 and quickly established himself, graduating to GPs within a few seasons. He enjoyed his greatest year in 1979, winning his first GP in the former Yugoslavia, four months after Valentino was born. Stefania gave birth on 16 February in Urbino, a few miles further into the

hills from Tavullia. Urbino was also birthplace of Rafael, one of the greatest painters of all time, and the walled Renaissance city has remained largely unchanged in half a millennium.

Graziano and Stefania had been married in October 1978 when Graziano was recovering from one of his crashes. The couple divorced in 1990. 'I think he only married me because he was confused!' smiles Stefania, who's now in another relationship and has a second son, Luca. 'We met at such a young age, I think that's why it didn't work.'

Rossi won another two 250 GPs in '79 for the local Morbidelli factory and was then snatched up by Suzuki to contest the following year's 500 World Championship. But a nasty rally car accident left him nursing head injuries and his career lost momentum. Nevertheless he managed to get a ride with Giacomo Agostini's Marlboro Yamaha team in 1982, which ended with a horrific 150mph crash at Imola. His career was over. 'I finish racing because I almost finish to be alive,' Graziano laughs at the dark moment, which renowned GP medic Dr Claudio Costa eased him

Graziano and three-year-old Vale, wearing dad's Drudi-designed lid, share some quality time. (Rossi archive)

Dig the leathers; and the number. Dad ran 46 when he won his first GP in 1979. Like father, like son. (Henk Keulemans)

Like Jesus, only faster. Graziano cut a certain dash in '79; still does today. (Henk Keulemans)

32

through. 'I was in coma for half day, I was Dr Costa's first miracle!'

Three-times 500 champ King Kenny Roberts remembers Rossi fondly, as a bit of a crasher. 'I recall one time he was scaring the shit out of me, and, of course, he ended up in a heap. I always knew that about him: "Okay it's Rossi, make sure you're not right on his ass coming out of this turn," you needed an exit plan, so I always gave him room.'

So Graziano was scary, but with a great mind and a heart of gold, according to former racing correspondent Barry Coleman. 'He rode like the wind and was a literary man, so we'd sit in his awning and discuss writers like Alberto Moravia (a 20th century Italian novelist). He'd say interesting things, like he'd wonder if racing was humane. He told me that whenever he saw someone crash he had a huge temptation to stop and help, which he had to repress; that's just too peculiar for a racer.'

Even if Valentino has no more than the haziest memory of his father's career, he now knows all about what Graziano got up to on the racetrack. When I told him about my own youthful regard for his dad, Valentino wanted to know why I was a fan. I said I liked the way Graziano could lead a GP by several seconds, then crash on the last lap. 'Yes, yes!' he replied, his face brightening in instant recognition. 'That's my father!'. On balance Valentino has done well out of his dad, inheriting some good genes and

benefiting from an upbringing rich in paternal warmth, intelligence and riding tuition.

Valentino had his first ride on a motorcycle when he was two and a bit. Neither father nor son remember what the bike was, but it came with outrigger safety wheels which lasted just three days. Surprise, surprise, he seemed to have a natural gift for it. 'He was pretty instinctive from the start,' says Graziano, who worked as a primary school teacher before his racing career took off. 'I was surprised by how little I had to explain, but I now think that kids of that age have more ability than we ever imagine.'

Stefania wasn't exactly thrilled to see Valentino getting into bikes but she too realised he was a natural. 'I could see that he wasn't dangerous, just from the way he was, the way he rode and I wasn't too protective as a mother,' she says. 'I was a lot more worried when Graziano raced! He made me too nervous, so I didn't go to many races.'

But Valentino did go to enough races to absorb the thrill of speed, colour and noise. Graziano remembers: 'After I retired I was friends with riders like (Loris) Reggiani and (Luca) Cadalora, so we'd go to grands prix to watch them. Valentino's first memories are of the paddock and when he was at home he played with motorbikes instead of other toys, this was just natural, he was never pushed. Around the age of four or five he was very curious and was surrounded by some great riders, so he'd always ask 2,000 questions to everyone,

The one that started it all; the outrigger wheels didn't stick around for long. (Rossi archive)

Dad Rossi's last
season, with
Marlboro Yamaha
in '82, ended with
a 150mph crash.
(Don Morley)

as any kid would do. People would disappear if they saw him coming, he was a pain in the ass at those times, but in general he was a bright and lovely kid.'

And pretty soon Valentino was trying to emulate his heroes. 'I remember my first big crash. It was '84 and I'd seen Randy Mamola hanging so far off his Honda 500 that his outside foot was off the footpeg. I went home and tried to do the same with my BMX bike and had a highside. Fack, I had a huge bruise and very much pain in the ass.'

So he was already getting a kick out of risk taking. Most kids take risks somehow, it's one way of finding out what they can get away with and how they relate to the world. One child might slap the face of a playmate, another might climb a tree, Rossi did daft things on bikes.

If mum wasn't much worried about their boy getting into motorcycles, Graziano was concerned. So he built him a go-kart, and not just any old go-kart. The chassis had been designed to take a 60cc grass-cutter motor and a ten-year-old driver, so Graziano bolted in a 100cc national kart motor and gave it to his five-year-old son. It was, dad remembers, 'an evil thing', and so fast that no one could stay with Valentino during their outings to local gravel pits. Here the gravel-pit gang – Rossi, Reggiani, Cadalora & Co. – would race around in beat-up rally cars, just for kicks. 'We had old Ford Escorts and Opel Asconas. We'd race around the pits and Vale was always faster in his kart.

The ground was great for learning, not so much grip so he'd be sideways all the time.'

Both Rossis have a passion for rallying and the gravel-pit gang still hang together today. 'We still go very often,' says dad. 'Me, Aldo (Drudi, racing's favourite graphic designer and the man behind both Rossis' helmet designs), Uccio (Vale's childhood mate and constant companion) and others, it's a nice way for friends to get together. Valentino is the only pro there and it's a big pleasure for us to watch him drive and do things. He grew up amongst racers, so it's always been with him, but there was no future seen in any of this, it was just fun, though maybe a bit dangerous.' Dangerous, for sure, but the kind of distraction that can stop kids growing up to be crackheads.

Meanwhile Valentino was getting on with primary school in Tavullia. Mum wanted him to grow up to be an engineer but while he was bright, he wasn't the most dedicated of pupils. 'He didn't used to feel like studying,' she remembers. 'But he had a great memory, so I'd read his school books to him while he lay on the couch and he'd get what he needed from that. He was a good kid, the kind that would get all the other kids together, his teachers always talked about that.'

If bikes and cars were the core of his childhood world, Valentino also showed a talent for guitar and football, although mother's efforts to take him to soccer school failed to distract him from his need for speed. And when his dad wasn't taking him to the

'What's with these guys; dodgy dancing?' The guitar was Vale's other big childhood love. (Rossi archive)

Inseparable from their school days: Vale (front right) and Uccio (standing behind in denim jacket). (Rossi archive)

gravel pits or to another GP, Vale would be sat in front of the TV, entranced by the great racers of the day. 'In F1 my heroes were Senna, Prost and Mansell, in bikes, Kevin Schwantz, Doriano Romboni and Loris Capirossi. Always Schwantz because he was the most spectacular and most beautiful on the bike, and also because of the colours. The style has always been important to me, and he was riding the Pepsi Suzuki then.' Even today the best compliment you can pay Valentino is to tell him that he rides like Schwantz. They both have an element of the cavalier in their riding and they've both got long, gangly, sticky-out legs.

Inevitably, the day came when Valentino wanted to go racing. He was nine at the time, a year too young for his junior kart licence but that wasn't going to stop the family from getting started. Remembering his own parents' refusal to sign for his racing licence, Graziano forged some documents with inside help from Tavullia's townhall, but their efforts were thwarted by a silly mistake. So Valentino had to wait.

Valentino was fast from the day of his very first race in early 1989, what a surprise. In 1990 he won the regional championship, enjoying his first victory that April, but by then he'd already spotted the toy he really, really wanted. 'The end of '89 was the start of the minimoto craze, there'd been nothing like minimoto before,' he says. 'As soon as I saw these bikes I wanted one, so I pushed and pushed my father until he bought me one. It was black, like Ron Haslam's Elf Honda.'

Right away it was obvious that this was what the boy really enjoyed: riding round and round in circles, grinding his kneesliders to dust, just like the big boys. And he wasn't the only one. It seemed like all the local kids had these Lilliputian racers which they'd thrash around the mini racetracks that pockmark the nearby seaside resorts of Rimini, Riccione and Cattolica. Not just the kids either, anyone could rent a minimoto for a few thousand lira any day of the week and pretty much any time of day or night. Teenagers would come tumbling out of the local nightclubs, well the worse for

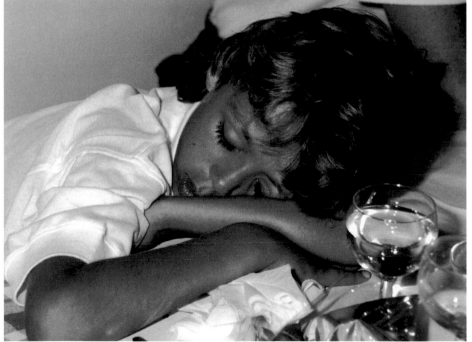

Down the gravel pits with his first kart, Valentino learns the basics of traction. (Rossi archive)

Sleep is still a big passion: 'When I wake up I have a big confusion!' (Rossi archive)

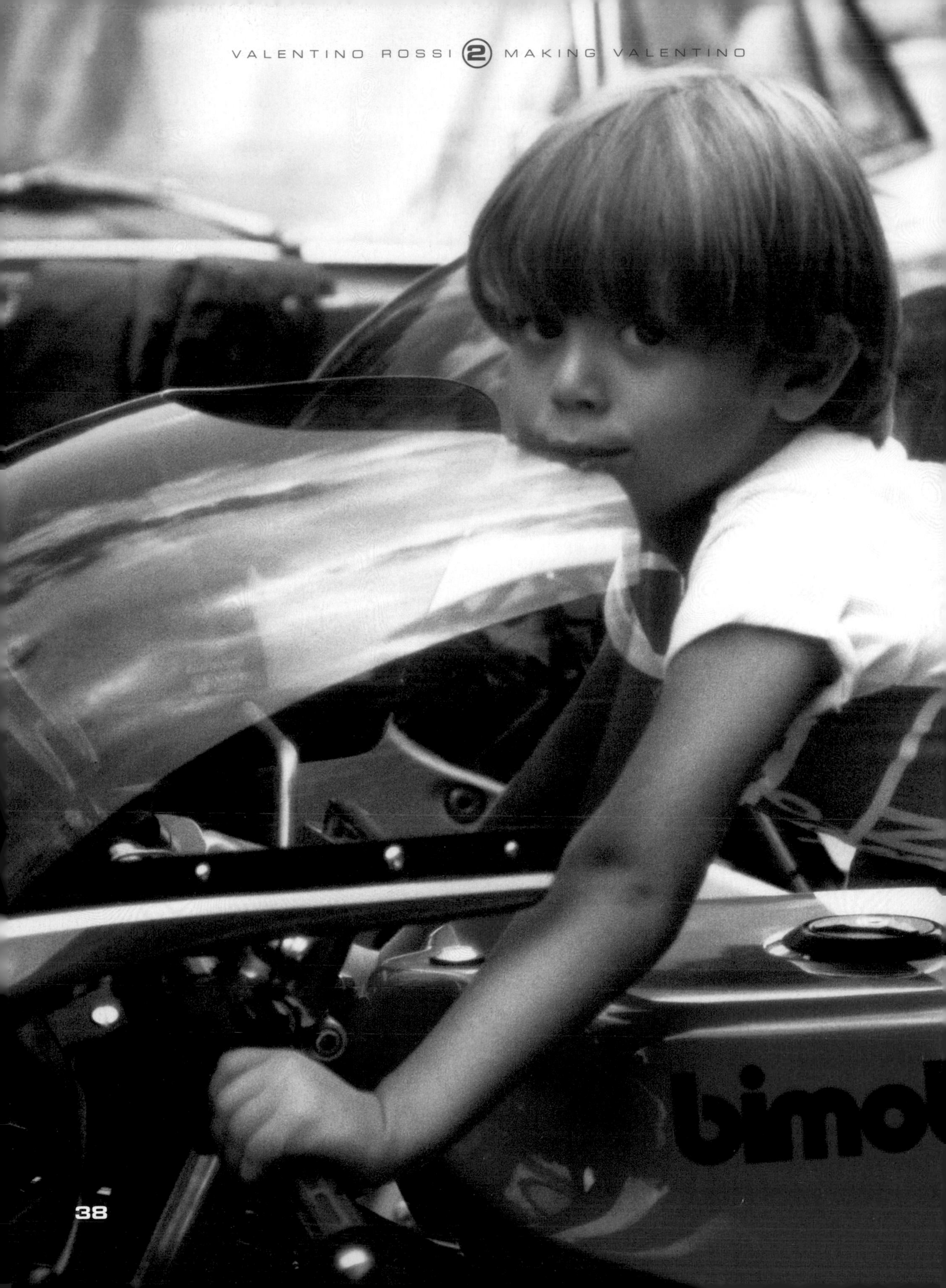
bimo

'When I grow up I'm going to be a bike racer.' Yes, course you are, Vale. (Rossi archive)

wear, and end up in a heap in the middle of some tiny racetrack, giggling until they puked. 'The whole area went crazy on minimoto, we used to ride them around tracks made for radio-controlled cars. At first it was four of us, then six, then 35, just riding around for fun, not proper racing.'

Vale wasn't the fastest of his gang, at least until the racing started for real. 'It was at Miramare in the summer of '91 and it must've been one of the first proper minimoto races. I remember it very well, the great atmosphere and the floodlights, because it was night. We used to ride at Cattolica on Wednesday evenings, then go to Miramare. There'd be so many people there, like a World Championship, because there were all the rent-a-racers too. There were 20 in the race and I was able to go away out front, it was a surprise because I'd never been fastest before.' Vale won another 15 races that summer, invariably running number 46, the number his dad had used to win his

first GP in '79, and wearing a Schwantz-replica Arai with a glued-on Ninja Turtle along for the ride. The Ninja Turtle fetish is still there – one of the creatures standing guard in his motorhome as he gets dressed before riding.

It's impossible to overestimate minimoto's crucial influence on the career of Rossi and his peers. 'You think of any Italian racer my age or a bit younger – Melandri, Poggiali, Sabbatani, Brannetti – they all came from minimoto. The first time I went to the track at Cattolica in December '89, Melandri was already there, he was only seven at the time but he was already a phenomenon.' Of course, Marco Melandri went on to succeed Rossi at Aprilia in 2000, Manuel Poggiali won the 125 world title in 2001 and both Max Sabbatani and Alessandro Brannetti got GP rides. 'Minimoto helped me very much. There would usually be four or five guys racing together, bumping into each other, so it taught me how to be aggres-

Vale learned to ride bicycles and motorcycles in dad's driveway. (Rossi archive)

sive, how to fight with other riders and how to overtake. Sometimes we raced in town squares, around tracks marked out by straw bales, so you'd have to learn to control the bike on bumps and slippery tarmac. It was difficult to overtake at some tracks, but I never had a problem.' He was already summoning up those weird lines that no one else even considered, showing the skills that would help him conquer the world.

And yet however hard he raced as a kid, Valentino's personality always shone through. He was already forging the characteristics that would serve him so well in adulthood and his mother soon recognised that he had a special attitude, unlike most kiddy racers who'd sulk or bawl whenever they got beaten. 'I was always impressed by how he always had fun with the whole thing,' says Stefania. 'He was really passionate about paddock life, he'd talk about that, or about battling with another rider, for days. He'd win one race, then

maybe lose another or crash, but he liked the whole thing, not just the winning.'

Stefania reckons Valentino hasn't changed in that respect. 'It's his easygoing attitude, it's not something he was taught. The things I really like about him are the personal stuff. If I had to tell you what's his best quality, it wouldn't be his riding talent.' But then she's his mum, she would say that. And yet talking to Stefania and Graziano it's obvious that both have an extra-special love for their son, there's huge warmth within this family unit, even if the parents split over a decade ago.

Following the divorce Vale moved in with his mum. 'Living with her was very much easier,' he recalls. 'My father always gave me a hard time if I came in late or something, but my mother never did that, she was much calmer. We were all happy though, because they still had a good relationship and lived near each other.'

Nonetheless Giampiero Sacchi, the man who gave

Okay, we get the picture, you've got the hang of it now. (Rossi archive)

Kid's kart racing in the town square; only in Italy. Valentino is number three. (Rossi archive)

Whatever, just so long as it's got an engine and some wheels. (Rossi archive)

Rossi his first GP ride in '96, believes the split may have had some kind of an effect on the youngster, albeit ultimately beneficial. He names two other recent champions to support his argument: Max Biaggi, whose parents split when he was very young, and Doohan, whose dad died when Mick was 11. Divorce can shatter lives but childhood troubles can strengthen some characters, giving them an inner strength, a spirit of independence. 'I've come to the conclusion that to be so strong in your life you probably need to have been in some difficult corners,' says Sacchi. 'I understood that when Valentino was doing 125s with me. These young guys are not living a normal life. A normal kid of 16 or 17 is okay thinking about school, he's not ready to think about racing 16 GPs, travelling all over the world and fighting for a World Championship. I don't know whether these guys are crazy or not, but sure they're special.'

Like Stefania, Graziano is also well aware of his son's special qualities. 'His approach to racing has always been the same. Even now when he has a bad

time in qualifying or he doesn't win the race, I see the same face that I sometimes saw when he was a kid, the tears lurking. He gets so involved and cares so much, he always has done, but he doesn't take it home. I think karts were a good schooling because he quickly learned how to lose, while he's always found it easy to be fast on bikes.'

Graziano likes to think he taught his son nothing, not through teaching anyway. 'I'm sorry about that,' he laughs. 'But I never had the chance to teach him anything because I quickly understood that he didn't want to hear my suggestions. Later on it got worse, if I suggested something he'd do the opposite! In general, parents can't teach their kids anything through words, it's from the way that they behave that kids pick up things. But there are some things I see in Valentino which I hope do come from me and that's his ability to have fun, to take things easy and not to dramatise life too much. Also, he wants to give the fans more than just a good race, and I hope he took that from me too. What I've learned from Valentino is

Thrashing along the driveway on his first minimoto – the bike that stopped him becoming a car racer. (Rossi archive)

The family that
plays together,
stays together.
Father and son in
the pits, Summer
'92. (Rossi
archive)

total straightforwardness and sincerity, even if these days those characteristics sometimes get him into awkward situations.'

Graziano sees one quality in his son which he knows he never had, and that's the champion's killer instinct. Any racer who thinks about pulling over when he sees someone crash obviously has a bit of a problem. To most racers, though they wouldn't admit it, a downed rider is just one less man to beat. It's a hard sport, people die and get crippled in motorcycle racing, and most riders have little room within themselves for sympathy or concern. It's a denial thing, if they opened up to others' suffering or the possibility of their own, they'd probably end up quitting. Sure, Valentino isn't your average racetrack psycho, he's a sweet and charming human being, but some kind of transformation obviously takes place within him when he's on the racetrack.

'There's one difference between myself and guys like Valentino, Doohan and Biaggi,' says Graziano. 'And that's the fact that I never won a World Championship! Valentino has this thing, the quality of a World Champion. When he shuts his visor and starts a race everybody becomes his worst enemy, he needs to fight these people and he needs to win. When I was racing I noticed that World Champions have this ability to shut off from the normal world. I didn't have that and that's why I don't have a World Championship.'

In cold psychological speak, Valentino has a Jekyll & Hyde character. No surprise there because there are plenty of nice guys racing motorcycles who are transmogrified the moment they ride down the pit lane. Until they return they are possessed, prepared to take the kind of risks, with their own lives and those of other people, which they'd never dream of taking in normal life (except, of course, when driving a rent-a-car). And yet these contrasting on-track and off-track characteristics aren't difficult to reconcile in Valentino's personality. It really is very simple: going fast is a gas and winning is a laugh, and while these actions require doing some pretty scary things, there's no requirement to bring the maniac with you when you climb off the bike. It's just that some racers get so wound up in it all that they forget that. 'If you win it's very much better,'

grins Valentino. 'But I never say to myself: "Ah fack, arriving in front is all that matters", I'm not obsessed. But, especially over the last two or three years, I know that I can win if I stay relaxed and concentrated. Maybe other riders like Biaggi are more angry with the other riders. I'm not angry with the other riders.'

So whatever Graziano says, it's obvious that he has taught his kid plenty. 'For sure I sometimes did the opposite of what my father told me,' admits Valentino. 'That's normal between father and son. If I make a mistake it's necessary that it's my own mistake. But he told me a lot of things and I often followed his advice. Whenever someone gives me advice I quickly decide whether it's bullshit or not. If it's not, I follow it.'

At the end of '91 father and son had an important decision to make. Rossi was still racing karts at this stage, minimotos were just for fun. He had finished fifth in that year's national kart championship at Parma and was ready to graduate to the Italian and European 100cc series in '92; the next step in a career that might have taken him all the way to F1. 'My plan was still for Valentino to race four wheels because I was scared he'd get hurt on a bike,' says Graziano. 'But two things changed this. First, he really, really liked minimoto, he used to spend all his days riding. Second, we realised that karts were getting too expensive for us, and we knew that car racing is all about money. If you don't have the best kart or car, you don't have much chance.'

Valentino takes up the story. 'We'd arrived at this point where we'd need 100 million lira for the '92 kart season, so I said to my father, "Maybe it's better we race with the bike," and he say "Ah, bo, really?". I say "Yes, so is it possible we race bikes?". He say "Yes,".'

So throughout '92 Vale, concentrating exclusively on minimoto racing, continued to learn the essentials of riding a motorcycle on tarmac just as fast as it'll go. 'But I was still just playing, not really thinking about the future. I wanted to win just like I wanted to win in karts, I think that's normal for a boy.' And win he did, all the way into '93, growing more serious about his racing by the day and growing taller too. It became apparent that soon he'd need a real motorbike.

Vale's mop raged
increasingly out of
control in '97.
The longer it
grew, the faster
he rode.
(Gold & Goose)

kids these days

Graziano Rossi's memory is a bit iffy at the best of times – blame a few too many bumps on the head – but he has a vivid recollection of his son's first race on a real motorcycle. And if all of dad's stories are scattered with laughter, this tale fills him with particular glee.

'We were at Maggione in spring of '93, practising for Valentino's first race on his Cagiva 125. He got on the bike, rode 100 metres out of the pit lane and crashed at the first corner. So he came back and we fixed the bike. An hour and a half later the bike was okay, so he rode down to the first corner, no problem, then second corner, crash!'

Graziano loves this story because, like most bike racers, he sees a harmless crash as something to laugh about, which makes two crashes so close together almost hilarious. Most of all though, he likes the story because of what happened right afterwards.

'When he got back to the pits we were thinking: "Are we doing the right thing here or are we making a big mistake putting him on a proper bike?" It wasn't so good. For sure, Valentino was also wondering if this was his job for the rest of his life, and there was an important look between us. We didn't exchange words but what I'd meant with that look was: "Yes, this can still be your job if you want, don't give up".' There he goes again, teaching without actually saying anything.

'You could see the disappointment in Valentino's eyes, he was almost crying. But these are the most important moments in a racer's career, when you find the strength to react and to show whether you're strong or you're weak.'

Valentino did indeed bounce back that weekend, finishing ninth in his first-ever race on a full-size bike.

Sometimes it hurts. Valentino makes his first visit to Dr Costa's clinic in '95. It wouldn't be his last. (Rossi archive)

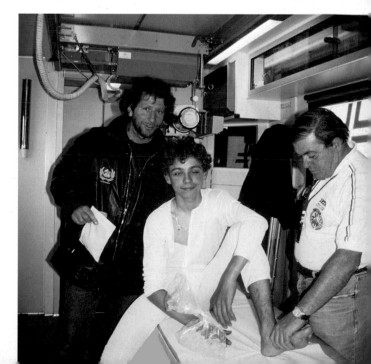

'Go on my son!'
Valentino has
just finished third
in the '93 Italian
Sport Production
series at Misano.
(Rossi archive)

The boy's a natural.
Vale graduated to
125 streetbikes in
'93, won the Italian
Sport Production
title in '94. The
usual one year to
learn, one year to
win. (Rossi archive)

Later on the world would see him perform similar comebacks time and again, until they became a defining feature of his career. He did it in his first 125 World Championship season, recovering from a rash of crashes to win his first GP, he did it in his first and second 250 campaigns, putting tumbles and miserable results behind him to go on to dominate. And he did it again when he graduated to 500s, dismissing two confidence-sapping get-offs to quickly assume mastery of racing's most challenging category.

There's obviously a pattern here, both in the cock-ups and the comebacks. 'It's a system,' says Valentino, explaining the crashes. 'Whenever I ride another kind of bike the beginning isn't fantastic, I make mistakes. I try to ride fast, I make mistakes, I need this to go faster.' It makes perfect sense, really. In racing there's only one way of locating the absolute limit and that's by tripping right over it. Once you've crashed you've found it, the next trick is to remember where it is, and a lot of racers never quite manage that part of the process.

Possibly even more miraculous than his ability to lock on to the limit, to the extent that he can dance along it all day, like he's taking a walk in the park, is his ability to stay cool when things go bad. 'Yes,' he says. 'This is very important, this is the key.' Again, many riders don't have this facility. Once they've started digging a hole for themselves they keep digging. It's just too easy to fall into this trap because racing is all about confidence and focus, and big, scary crashes tend to destroy both, unravelling even the greatest of talents. Probably it is only the real greats who can recover from such situations, but who knows how they manage that, via a Zen-like inner state or sheer bloody mindedness? 'I don't know how,' offers Valentino. 'Just that I've had some difficult periods but so far I've arrived at all my targets.' His Honda engineer Jerry Burgess begs to differ: 'Determination is the thing that unites the champions, that and a real fear of getting beaten.'

So he was rightly delighted with his ninth place at Maggione, although he remembers that crunching first day of practice somewhat differently from his father, and this isn't the only time their memories conflict. 'Yes, I crashed at the first corner but next time I made three or four laps before I crash.' In mitigation he adds:

'It was early morning, very cold, and new tyres.'

The race was the first round of that year's 125 Italian Sport Production Championship, open to hotted-up 125 streetbikes like Valentino's Cagiva Mito. This wasn't the first man-sized bike he'd ridden though. The previous summer he'd sneaked out at Misano, riding a mate's Aprilia SP racer. 'I was still too young to go on a real racetrack, so it had to be secret. My friend signed on, then I wore his leathers. This was my first time on a proper bike and a proper racetrack, it was like a dream.'

Valentino didn't set the world alight in 1993. He made more mistakes, of course, but by season's end he was quick enough to take pole position at the Misano finale and finish the race third behind Andrea Ballerini and Roberto Locatelli. Both these men moved into GPs before Rossi, Locatelli going on to capture the 2000 125 world title.

The following year was very different. Rossi had an official Mito, supplied by Cagiva team manager Claudio Lusuardi, with which he recorded his first national victory at Monza. By the Misano finale he only needed a third-place finish to claim the title. 'I was third into the last corner but Stefano Cruciani arrive much too fast and knock me wide because he's facking crazy. I finish fourth, then they disqualify him, so I am the champion.' Cruciani, by the way, never made it to GPs. During '94 Rossi also became acquainted with life on slicks, contesting the Italian 125 GP series aboard a Sandroni, an Aprilia-engined special built by Pesaro engineer Guido Mancini, the engine provided by Aprilia race chief Carlo Pernat, an old mate of Graziano's.

So he was getting pretty busy with his racing, which didn't leave much time for school. If he wasn't playing truant to go riding, he was struggling just to get out of bed in the mornings, a habit that would stay with him into his first year of 500s when he famously slept through morning practice at the Catalan GP. His love of the lie-in compelled him to find a new way of getting to school and he hit on the idea of using the family's Ape car, a rather comical three-wheeled pick-up powered by a desperately overworked scooter motor. Stefania remembers: 'Getting the bus to secondary school meant he'd have to get up earlier, so he'd wake up at the last minute, grab the Ape and fly

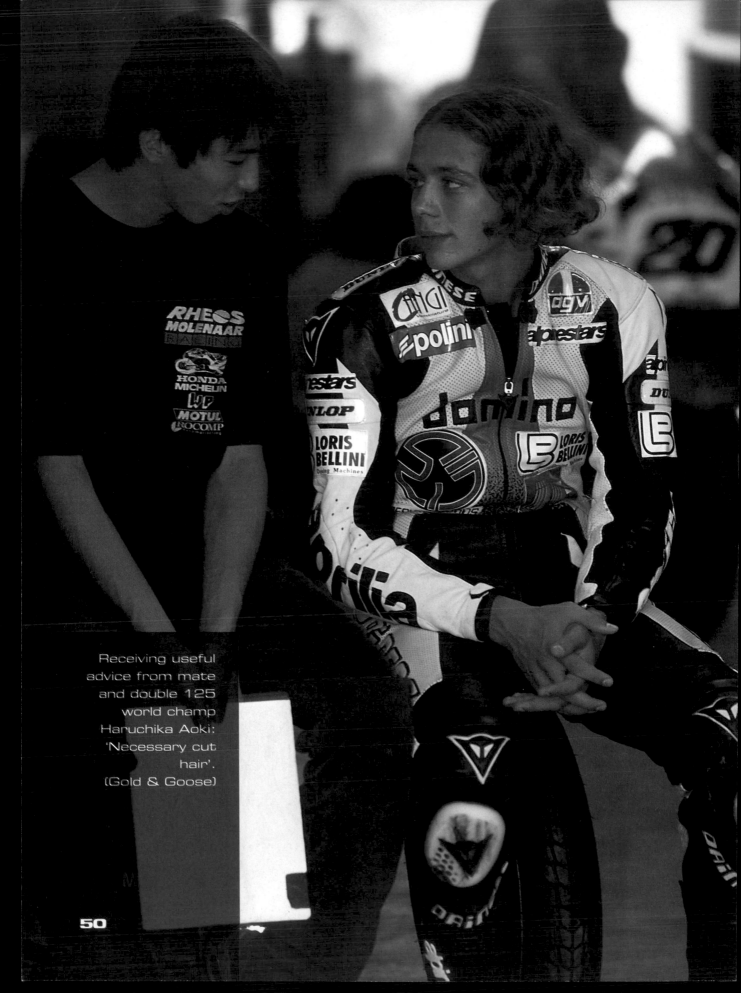

Receiving useful advice from mate and double 125 world champ Haruchika Aoki: 'Necessary cut hair'. (Gold & Goose)

down the hill to Pesaro.' Soon all his friends had Apes. 'At first, everyone looked at me like I was an idiot but the Ape became our gang's official means of transport, we even used them to go to the disco!' Once again Valentino was showing a tendency to stand out from the crowd,

And of course, all this youthful exuberance got him into trouble with the local police. 'There was a time when Valentino, his friends and their scooters caused total panic around this area,' says Graziano, a proud dad's grin spreading across his face. Nothing serious, mind. 'They were always getting chased by the cops, and at one time it was like open war between them, they really hated each other. They got chased down a dirt road and the police car ended up in a ditch.' You can imagine the scene, straight out of a Keystone Cops movie: the cop car teetering on its side, steam rising from beneath the bonnet and the sweating Carabinieri in their bulging tunics and pompous hats, shaking fists and screaming obscenities. In fact, this is another case of father's and son's memories diverging. Valentino doesn't remember the incident, but even if this is Graziano's memory playing tricks on him, it's too good a fantasy to remain untold. This is what Valentino remembers: 'We were racing along the road from Pesaro to Cattolica on our scooters, like we always did, and suddenly we arrived at this police road block. I tried to escape by diving down a dirt road and crashed. So I kept quiet and waited for the police to go away but they didn't, so eventually I came

out with my hands up. The problem was that they were looking for people with drugs, so they wanted to know why I'd been so keen to get away.'

His father goes on: 'That kind of thing is pretty normal around here. The good thing was that Valentino's group of friends were very close, this was just a big adventure for them. Getting chased by the cops and getting tickets was a downside, but they looked after each other, made sure no one got into real trouble.' Vale didn't survive his scooter days totally unscathed, however. In the summer of '94 he grabbed a lift to the beach with a mate, a car pulled out in front of them, breaking his left ankle and mangling a couple of toes.

If his racetrack results didn't yet put him head and shoulders above his rivals, he'd done enough to further prick the interest of Aprilia, who were signing a certain Max Biaggi to their 250 GP team at the same time. Pernat had liked Vale from their first meeting. 'I like him,' he says from behind his rarely removed black-out shades, 'because he remind me of Kevin Schwantz.' Aprilia provided a standard RS125R for the 1995 Italian and European championships and it was during those six months that Valentino came of age as a roadracer. He dominated the Italian series from the outset and made his first forays abroad.

'I think '95 was the best-ever European series because the races were run at the GPs. It was good because the GP riders would practice, then we'd be on the same track a few hours later, so we could compare. I watched all the 125

There was still plenty to learn, of course. Vale goes low flying in France. (Gold & Goose)

GP sessions and races.' During his travels he struck up a friendship with Japanese 125 GP rider Haruchika Aoki, who won the 1995 and '96 125 World Championships and then moved to 250s and 500s. 'I had always had a passion for Japanese riders because I was very much into graphics and colours. They seemed to come from another world, with crazy helmet designs and very different leathers. Both me and Haruchika used Diadora boots that year, that's how we got introduced, and every time we went to another track he would take me around for a lap and tell me important things. That was fantastic.' And this was the year that Valentino's first alter-ego was born. Rossi became Rossifumi, after wild-riding Japanese 500 star Norifumi Abe.

Aoki's teachings may have been vital but they took a while to sink in. Rossi spent much of his time abroad limping in and out of Dr Claudio Costa's Clinica Mobile, the travelling hospital that looks after GP racing's walking wounded. 'In the Euros I was always racing Lucio Cecchinello who had an HRC-kitted Honda which was impossible to beat. But I wanted to beat him, so I'd go, go, go, and after, crash, crash, crash.' Nevertheless he finished the series third, enough to guarantee him entry to the following year's 125 World Championship.

This time Rossi did a deal with Giampiero Sacchi, racetrack kingmaker, collector of old Gileras and a lyrical teller of racing tales. 'At that time I was Biaggi's manager and the idea came to me to make a team for the '96 World Championship,' says Sacchi, who later guided Manuel Poggiali to the 2001 125 title. 'I couldn't afford a big rider, so I came to an agreement with Valentino

and his father. It was a good team with standard bikes but very enthusiastic and even then Valentino was Valentino. I'd never seen a rider who wanted to do things like fix all the stickers to his bike. He's always been very careful with the details, that was the first shock!'

Sacchi wasn't the only one in for a shock. First time Rossi shared a racetrack with his GP heroes was during pre-season tests at Jerez in southern Spain. 'Fack, it was incredible, they were so fast! It was like another sport, maybe four seconds a lap faster. I thought I would never be able to ride like that, I needed to learn another way to ride the bike.'

And learn he did. The '96 season started at Malaysia's old GP venue, Shah Alam, a tortuous track that winds its way through encroaching tropical jungle. Rossi finished a creditable sixth in his GP debut and followed that with reasonable enough rides to 11th in Indonesia and Japan. Back on familiar ground at Jerez for the start of the Continental sector of the championship he was bang on the pace – on the front row for the first time and in the thick of a typically crazed ten-man battle for the lead. 'I was second out of the final corner but I crossed the line fourth, and exactly the same happened at the next race at Mugello. My bike was very slow, I had many good races that year, but also some big, crazy mistakes.'

Indeed, Rossi suffered more than 15 crashes during 1996. He was a young man in a hurry, too much of a hurry after missing the podium by a fraction in Spain and Italy. Desperate for his first pop at the post-race champagne, he crashed out of the next two races in

'Vale, how is it possible you crash so much?' Giampiero Sacchi has a quiet word, Assen '96. (Henk Keulemans)

Already working on the royal wave. Vale's first podium, Austria '96, with winner Ivan Goi. (Gold & Goose)

'I thought I could win, now I just think I'm an idiot.' Valentino bales out, Suzuka '97. (Henk Keulemans)

The merry
prankster comes
out to play after
another win, this
time in France.
(Henk Keulemans)

Showing them
how it's done.
Vale heads for his
fifth win of the
year at Assen...
(Gold & Goose)

...and is
miraculously
transformed into
Superfumi! (Gold
& Goose)

France and Holland, although not before he'd secured his first GP lap record at Ricard. 'It was necessary for me to ride crazy because my bike was so slow, and when you ride like this all the time, it's possible you crash. At Assen it was damp, I started 20th and after three laps I was second, then crash. Crazy!'

That accident brought matters to a head within Sacchi's tightly budgeted little outfit. 'You can imagine that all these crashes weren't good for the team,' Sacchi recalls. 'Many came from Vale just not thinking; the tyres: cold! Give gas: crash! So we take him into the motorhome and I say: "Vale, how is it possible you crash so much?". But now I understand there are many riders who don't crash and who never make it. The lesson is this: if a young rider is very fast, he's going to crash. He needs to discover the limit, and without crashing it's impossible to find the limit.'

Rossi remembers that little chat in the motorhome like it was yesterday. 'I remember Sacchi's words, he say to me: "If you continue like this, the maximum possible is that you become like Kevin Schwantz [who had recently been forced into retirement by aching injuries], but if you want to become like Max Biaggi [then riding the crest of a wave in the 250 class], it's necessary you change." So I say to myself: "Fack, I continue like

this!".' The Rossi/Biaggi agro may have been far in the future, but Valentino already knew he didn't like the 250 champ, Biaggi was too proud, too Roman for his liking. You only need to take a look at www.valentinorossi.com to guess what he thinks of him: Biaggi's name never even appears, just XXX XXXXX.

Despite all the tumbles, Valentino's speed hadn't gone unnoticed. Aprilia were impressed enough to give him some factory parts; a better cylinder and a carbon front disc brake, because he was shattering the standard steel discs. The trick gear made all the difference: third in Austria for his first podium, then his first pole position and win at Brno in the Czech Republic. Rossi had arrived.

At Brno he beat veteran 125 champ Jorge Martinez by a fraction after a frenzied final few laps. Martinez, like many of the older GP racers, greatly disapproved of the kamikaze tactics employed by these crazy minimoto-drilled kids. The Spaniard had started his long and illustrious World Championship career way back in '82 when racing was less frantic, if only because there weren't so many good bikes around back then. He even remembers seeing Graziano's toddler in the paddock, and ruefully remarked after his defeat: 'I should've taken my chance then and run him over'.

Sacchi, of course, had seen it all before. 'It's like a

pack of wolves, a new leader arrives, pushes the limit and the old leader has to give way. When Valentino arrived at the front, Martinez said that his riding was dangerous, and people said the same thing when Poggiali arrived.' Martinez retired a year later.

Rossi should've won more races in 1996. 'But after Brno the bad luck came. I was leading at Imola when the facking sparkplug broke, then Tokudome took me out at the first turn at Barcelona. At Rio I had a bad crash in practice which gave me a problem with my shoulder, so I crashed again in the race. In Australia another 'plug break.'

All this was of little consequence, however, because Brno had rocked Rossi's world. Now he knew he was more than just part of the pack and that changed his whole perspective on racing. 'Until you win you don't know you can win.' Sounds obvious, doesn't it?. 'And the win made me more happy because I think maybe it's possible I can win some more.'

For '97 Rossi was afforded the full-factory treatment by Aprilia: a pair of expensively honed factory

By Imola the Rossi phenomenon had gripped most of Italy. Vale dropped by to say 'Hi!' (Gold & Goose)

Who's the kid in the Porsche? Vale blags a ride around the awesome 14-mile Nürburgring. (Milagro)

RS125Rs and a factory crew headed by Mauro Noccioli, Sacchi still fronting the effort. And it wasn't just the equipment and personnel that were better, Rossi was also new and improved, no longer a GP dreamer, now he knew he could win this thing.

'I had a very good bike for '97 so I knew in my heart that I could win. Winning the championship wasn't a surprise, though winning 11 races and not making too many mistakes was. Before '97 I always made mistakes – I had more than 20 crashes in '95, 15 in '96 and maybe only three in '97. I changed because when you understand your power you become more confident and with more engine you can be more relaxed. The better bike also helped my concentration because when you've got a slow bike you push too hard and sometimes lose concentration. And after you crash, crash, crash you say to yourself: "Fack, it's better I don't crash" because the asphalt is very hard.'

Sacchi was well aware of the change that came over his young protégé that winter. 'His mind changed, he became another person, but maybe the biggest change happened when he won the first race in Malaysia, then he realised he could win all of them. He

was now sure of himself inside, he had the conviction, something that normal riders don't have. For me '97 was a dream, like being in paradise.'

Rossi messed up only once all season, tumbling out of round two at Suzuka while planning a last-lap push for victory. 'I thought I could win, now I just think I'm an idiot,' he said after wandering back to pit lane, grinning all the way and waving to the crowd. Even when he was beaten he appeared unbeaten. On the few occasions he was defeated in '97 he giggled his way through the podium ceremony just like he'd won, so his Japanese rivals couldn't nurture a hatred of the guy that might help them push just a little harder. Nobby Ueda (who won the other four races), Tomomi Manako, Kazuto Sakata and Masaki Tokudome could do nothing but laugh with him. Maybe Vale wasn't conscious of what he was doing, but these days he seems more aware of the psychological benefits of grinning when he's not winning, denying Biaggi & Co. the pleasure of seeing him well and truly vanquished.

Ninety-seven was the year Rossi mania grabbed everyone, when he began the winning that allowed him to indulge his kink for dressing up and showing people a good time. He looked no less ridiculous out of his post-race fancy dress, his girly mop raging increasingly out of control as the season went on, especially when soaked in that stinking podium cocktail of warm champagne and sweaty leathers. At times the mane was kept vaguely in check by a girl's Alice band, and finally, after he'd secured the title, it was chopped off, the new and much tidier coiffure dyed blue with a blond number 1 at the back.

The fun and games began after he scored his third victory of the year at Mugello. If he was going to make the effort anywhere, he might as well do it there, where the Italian fans go to extraordinary lengths to get involved and make some noise. The most ardent of them bring along static, open-piped engines which are deployed on the hillsides surrounding the Tuscan track and then rev them to oblivion, joined now and again by bikers caning their own motors until they rat-a-tat-tat off their rev limiters. Fireworks, thunderflashes and hundreds of camp fires complement the megaphone madness to forge a war-zone ambience. 'Up on the hill

it's another world, the crowd is coming crazy: drink, naked people on motocross bikes, it's crazy! I was up there in '96 when I wasn't so well known and blew up someone's CBR engine, ooops! In '97 I went up in the evening and it was very dangerous, everyone jumping on me, shouting 'Rossi! Rossi!'. There was this big wall of people and only one way out, through the shower block, so I rode my scooter through the shower block. If I hadn't, I'd probably still be up there now.'

So how was he going to entertain this bunch of crazies? In recent years it had become the fashion for winning riders to stop on the slowdown lap and find an obliging track-invading fan with the appropriate national flag. 'If I won I didn't want to do that, I wanted to ride around with something different.' So halfway through his victory lap he stopped by his fan club's encampment and rode on accompanied by a blow-up Claudia Schiffer. The doll had been in its wrapping for nine months: in case of victory, open box.

'Gibo and me bought the doll before Imola '96 but, fack, I didn't win there, so it stay in box until we win at Mugello. But the Claudia idea wasn't mine because this talk about the Biaggi thing with her hadn't happened when we got the doll, it was my fan club's idea to write Claudia Schiffer on the back!' The gag poked fun at Biaggi's rumoured liaison with Naomi Campbell. The relationship between Italy's favourite two racers, such as it was, had deteriorated after Rossi had a go at Max on an Italian TV chat show, Biaggi fronting up to him in a Suzuka restaurant, saying: 'Stay quiet, I am number one.' Rossi's new profile had brought his feelings for Max into the open and the Italian media were in like Flynn. Asked by one shit-stirring journalist if he considered himself the Biaggi of the 125s, he cheekily replied: 'No, Biaggi is the Rossi of the 250s!' From now on the pair would be rival suitors for the affections of the Italian public, the opposing armies of fans colour coded for easy identification: Marlboro red for Biaggi, yellow for Valentino, his favourite colour.

Next time out in Austria Ueda cancelled the party, by four thousandths of a second, but normal service was resumed in France (minstrel's hat on the podium) and Holland (a carefully customised plastic Superman-style Rossifumi cape). At Imola, where he achieved his third straight win, he left it to his fans to indulge in some straightforward crowd anarchy – the hillside opposite the pits ablaze with yellow fan club T-shirts and giant cut-out letters proclaiming ROSSIFUMI COSMICO. From here on in, it was *Il fenomeno Rossi* all the way.

More wins followed in Germany (medieval torturer, swinging a mace), Britain (Robin Hood, brandishing a kid's bow and arrow), and Rio to make it six in a row. Late in August he wrapped up the title at Brno, three races still to go. He still counts that day the best of his many great days. 'Becoming World Champion is for sure the greatest moment and maybe the first one was best. That and the 500, because it was the 500.'

A month later in Indonesia, he won his 12th and last 125 GP, dancing on to the podium wearing a comedy

Ready for some scooter mayhem in Tavullia's piazza. The middle house in the background has since been painted bright yellow in homage to Valentino. (Aprilia)

'This weekend I will be mostly Robin Hood'. Donington's near Nottingham, you see. (Gold & Goose)

61

All bandaged up with no place to go after his final 125 win at Sentul, where he beat Sakata. (Gold & Goose)

head bandage. The previous weekend he'd been celebrating the championship in Tavullia and the night went all rock star on him: a few drinks, a couple of girls and a car crash. 'My popularity had gone from zero to huge, my life went from normal to not normal, so we made a big party with the fan club. Afterwards we went to a disco in Montecchio. We had two cars and there was a girl in one car and another girl in the other. For sure, whichever car I went in, the girl in the other car would be angry, so me, my father and Loris got into another car, a Porsche 928. On the way Graziano wanted to try the car, so we went to this industrial estate. I was in the back, on the phone, when Graziano started getting sideways, but he exited one corner too fast and it was a big crash. We took out a lamp post, I hit my head and had some problems in the night.'

The Italian papers went huge on the story. 'And they all wrote that I was driving the car. It was a big, big casino (Italian for row), fack, incredible!' This was Rossi's first experience of the dark side of the media and it shook him up. 'I was very, very angry, it was a big shock.' Until then he'd been more sociable with the media than any other rider, whiling away hours on Sunday evenings laughing and joking with journalists in circuit media centres. Maybe he'd been trying to get on the right side of the oh-so-fickle Italian press, although it really had looked like he was just having some fun. From now on, however, he'd be more suspicious of their intentions.

The two sides of Valentino; his racing yin and yang. (Gold & Goose)

At the same time he was discovering another downside to fame – the impossibility of even walking down the street without getting jumped on. When he visited that autumn's Milan bike show the organisers armed him with a couple of security gorillas. 'But they pushed the fans around and I didn't like that.' So what to do for the big show at Bologna? 'I dressed up with dark shades, a wig like Ruud Gullit and a baseball cap. I looked just like another fan and didn't get hassled once all day.'

Of course, he only had himself to blame for being too much adored. So does he ever regret having played the showoff? 'Sometimes, but I think I give good fun to people, though most of all to myself. I love doing new things, like the nac nac (a precarious wheelie performed standing with only one foot on the 'pegs). In 2000 I make very much rolling burnout, in 2001 I make very much nac nac, it's always necessary to learn something new. Nowadays I'm still happy when I win, as happy as '97, but there's less time to organise things. Always the ideas are mine, except Robin Hood, that was Gibo. My favourite one? For sure the doll!'

The doll was funny, supremely silly but funny, and if some of the other gags were almost painfully contrived there seemed no harm in it. This was just an ingenuous teenager enjoying himself, determined to squeeze maximum fun out of every moment. And now that he'd squeezed maximum fun out of GP racing's kindergarten, he needed somewhere new to play…

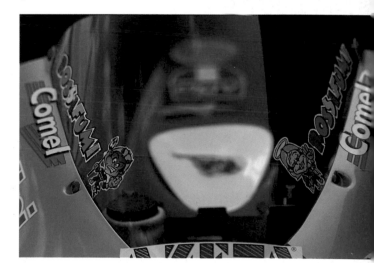

'You calling me a chicken?' Valentino and friend celebrate at Catalunya '98, scene of the third of his 14 250 wins. (Gold & Goose)

doing the funky chicken

But was he really any good? The racetracks of the world are littered with the broken hopes of have-a-go 125 heroes who never quite developed their skills to meet the greater, nastier demands of 250 and 500 racing; demolished fairings, fractured bones, shattered careers. In 125s, being a psychopath is almost enough. If you're braver and madder than the other guys, you might just succeed, if only on those occasions when you don't end up in an agonised heap by the side of the track. Relatively speaking, talent and intelligence aren't essential to racing a puny 45 horsepower 125.

Valentino might not be any different. So far there'd been little indication that we might be witnessing the creation of an all-time great, because all he'd done was ride a 125 very well. But Aprilia were pretty sure they'd got hold of someone special, someone who would

more than recompense them for the loss of the man who'd put the little Italian concern on the motorcycling map. Max Biaggi had quit Aprilia under a storm cloud at the end of 1996, defecting to Honda, whom he hoped would look after him when he was ready to graduate to 500s. The Roman did what was expected of him, wresting the 250 crown from his old employers and presenting it to Honda, who kept their part of the bargain, furnishing him with a brace of NSR500s for 1998. So the much awaited Valentino v Biaggi showdown would have to wait a while longer…

Aprilia determined to nurture their new asset like a favoured son. They assigned Valentino one of their greatest pit-lane engineers, the squat, avuncular Rossano Brazzi, who had worked with Aprilia's original GP hero Loris Reggiani. Over the next two years Brazzi

Aprilia's brothers blue – Vale's first year in 250s, with team-mates Capirossi and Harada, was spoiled by infighting within the Italian squad. (Milagro)

Just popping
down the beach.
Displaying a talent
for gloriously
inappropriate
clothing after
riding to second
at Mugello '98.
(Henk Keulemans)

and Valentino would build a special relationship that continues today. 'We still have fun together,' Brazzi says. 'We meet up when he's back in Italy and go out for dinner. Most of these evenings end up the way they always used to, with the restaurant getting trashed.'

Brazzi was perfect for Vale: a dedicated technician but a warm and gentle human being, so unlike the cold-blooded, data-fixated brainboxes who populate some stretches of pit lane. And he knew exactly what he was dealing with from the word go. 'The quality of Valentino was evident from the first time I worked with him at Jerez at the end of '97,' recalls Brazzi. 'That was the first time he rode the 250 and he broke the lap record!'

So right away Valentino had proven that he was more than just a 125 nutter, and not just with his riding skill but also with his guile. He was only 18 at the time and yet he knew the eyes of the racing world would be upon him when he rolled up for his first ride. He therefore wanted to make sure he made a real impression, a psychological impact, so he got on to the Dunlop guys and asked them to bring some super-soft qualifying tyres. At the end of the tests he comfortably surpassed the 250 record. All of a sudden he was faster than Biaggi.

Fortuitously, Valentino entered the 250 arena when Aprilia were at the height of their powers in the class. The RSW had long been the fastest 250 but that year it enjoyed a greater-than-ever advantage, because Honda's engineers had got their sums badly wrong with a brand-new NSR250. The '98 NSR was a dog,

nothing more, nothing less. And not only did Aprilia enjoy superior speed, they'd also assembled their strongest-ever team, Valentino lining up alongside his childhood hero Loris Capirossi and the similarly experienced Tetsuya Harada. Harada had won the 250 world title at his first attempt in '93 and would almost certainly have been further decorated if he hadn't suffered some miserable luck. Capirossi had been the proto-Valentino, the first of GP racing's teen stars, when he won the 1990 125 crown at 17. The toothy, hard-riding Italian from Riolo Terme, an hour's drive from Valentino's hometown, had retained the title in '91 and graduated to 250s the following year.

Thus Vale seemed to be in an ideal situation: fast bikes and fast team-mates, so no pressure to succeed too soon. Not so. 'All the other bikes were shit but I had two foxes for team-mates, both with many years of 250 experience, and the atmosphere in Aprilia was terrible. All the chief mechanics were fighting, you know, it was an Italian team: "Ah you have the best cylinder", this and that and so on. For me it was difficult to ride like Loris and Harada because they have more experience, but I didn't want to arrive third behind them, because to arrive third was to arrive last.'

And yet there were reasons to be happy he'd made the move, rather than indulging himself by carrying the 125 number-one plate. 'Maybe the best thing about 250s was that I could get out of bed later! I had to get up at seven for 125 practice, and that was a big problem

Leading Capirossi and Harada at Ricard. Aprilia's speedy threesome spent most of '98 formation fighting, well ahead of any rivals. (Gold & Goose)

for me, in 250s I could stay in bed until nine.'

Comfy lie-ins notwithstanding, Valentino cites 1998 as the toughest and therefore most important year of his career. Just as it was Mick Doohan's injury-wracked '89 GP season that tempered the Aussie into an indomitable racetrack warrior, so it was '98 that helped make Valentino the man he is today, although his suffering wasn't so much physical as psychological. He was having trouble distinguishing his real mates from an ever-burgeoning gang of hangers-on and dealing with the deaths of two of his best friends in a car accident.

'It was the most difficult year for me, because everyone expected so much and I really felt the pressure. I was fast but I made mistakes because I wasn't relaxed. I had some personal problems with some friends who weren't real friends. It was like a balloon, it got bigger and bigger, then it had to burst. There were too many people around who only stayed with me because I'm Valentino and I didn't understand this very quickly because it was something new. I needed some time to understand and then I realised why I wasn't concentrating on racing. My level went down all year, until we hit the bottom at Brno.'

The racing started at Suzuka, where bike problems kept him out of the running. He was quickly realising that 250s were altogether tougher, requiring intricate set-up work. 'Unlike 125s, everything must be just perfect or you have no chance of getting on the podium, let alone winning. Also, I missed my friends in

125s, though in my first qualifying session I saw that there are just as many crazy guys in 250s!'

Valentino would find out just how crazy when the circus headed south for the Malaysian GP, staged for one year only at Johor, just across the border from Singapore. Wearing a new skinhead cut for the subtropical heat, he was right on it, qualifying on the front row for the first time and racing for the lead with Harada and Honda's Tohru Ukawa. Just a few corners to go and he was ahead but Harada stuffed it up the inside at the final turn, robbing the youngster of the grippy line and forcing him on to the dirtier tarmac. The crash was a big one. 'Maybe I should've let him pass but after leading I couldn't do that. As the Japanese say: "Necessary make win!".' The race wasn't the only thing he lost that weekend – a reckless bet with Capirossi cost him a further million lira. All his team-mate had to do was risk his life by jumping off a hotel walkway into the pool, a 12-metre drop with no run up.

On to Europe and another two crashes during Spanish GP practice suggested that Valentino was retracing his 125 GP learning curve – fast, furious and often floored. But Jerez also commenced a strong run of results, his first 250 points for a hard-ridden second behind Capirossi, and another vital lesson learned. 'I'd geared my bike for the fastest-possible lap; that's what I used to do in 125s because you could run the same speed all race. But that's not possible in 250s: the tyres slide very much, so you go slower through the corners, so your gearing ends up too high.'

Second again at Mugello and Paul Ricard, he arrived at hot 'n' dusty Jarama, outside Madrid, in mid-June, convinced he was ready to win. Once again he did lead, as he'd done at Johor, Mugello and Ricard, and once again he jumped off. If he thought the press would cut him some slack during his apprenticeship, he was very wrong. He'd made a few mistakes on track and now he would make his first off it: naively under-estimating the fickleness of the media and his fans. 'Very many journalist, who I thought were my friends, said: "Rossi won very many 125 races but 250s aren't the same and he's made mistakes, he's stupid". This was really bad for me, but also really good because I found out who my real friends were. Before then I thought I had more friends than I actually did.'

He also copped plenty of flack for his post-race jinks at Mugello, where he stopped on the slowdown lap and changed into beach gear, riding back to the podium ceremony in flip-flops. 'People said bad things about that. It's like if you win every race of your career you're a genius, but if you finish second you're a facking clown!'

Despite the media casino, Valentino was having as much fun as ever between races; playing football and racing minimoto, motocross and radio-controlled cars with Melandri, who'd just started his first 125 GP season. His weakest point was motocross. 'So I'd ring Marco, tell him we don't need to ride today, then do a few hours riding in secret!'

The nights were just as hectic. 'The Saturday before Jarama we went to a crazy club in Riccione – a lot of people out of their minds, really high, it's incredible what the young do for enjoyment! And I nearly got into a fight. This guy asked me for a cigarette and I told him I don't smoke, so he asked me again, then he said: "You won't give me a cigarette because you're Rossi," he wanted a fight!'

There were other reasons he needed bigger muscles. 'I never did any proper training when I was riding 125s because the bikes are like bicycles. Then at the end of '97 everyone said I need to go to the gym to be stronger for the 250, but I don't go because I don't like. At Jarama it's very bumpy, I wasn't in control of the bike, that's when I understood I need more power. So my mentality changed, I started going to the gym and now it's one of my passions, if I don't go for some days I get frustrated. I think I'm in good shape now, with very much more power than two years ago.'

The weekend before the Dutch GP, the season's halfway point, Valentino and some of his real mates scootered six miles down the road to play the fan at the Misano World Superbike round. 'It was like being a kid again, we just laid in the grass by the side of the track, sunbathed and watched the racing.' And in the evening he joined Yamaha's larger-than-life Supers hero Noriyuki Haga for some serious drowning of sorrows. The Japanese had crashed out of both races that day and astonished Vale with his drinking ability.

Getting it right at last (the 250, not the hair colour). Valentino's first 250 win came at Assen. (Henk Keulemans)

Defeating
boredom between
practice sessions
at the
Sachsenring.
(Milagro)

Assen next and the big breakthrough. His hair dyed bright orange for the occasion, although unaware of the colour's significance to the Dutch crowd, he motored into the lead 'like I was in a plane' and won by 20 seconds. Capirossi and Harada both stopped with bike problems.

Brazzi was impressed: 'It took Valentino half a season to get used to the 250. The biggest problem that most riders face when they move up from 125s is that 250s move around more, they're more nervous, both on the power and in their general handling behaviour. Initially, that nervousness gave him some problems; he didn't like it when the bike started sliding around, but he soon understood that's the way it is, and after a while he realised that just because the bike is sliding doesn't mean he's going to crash. Then he understood how to use the sliding to his advantage, just as he did in 500s.'

His team-mates' Assen DNFs brought Valentino to within 19 points of series leader Harada, although he hardly dared believe he was ready to race for the title. Just as well, because he crashed again at Donington, caught out by a full tank of gas and hard race tyres. It was the end of a miserable weekend, Italy crashing out of the football World Cup on Friday night.

In Germany, two weeks later, he was a chastened third behind winner Harada and Jeremy McWilliams's privateer Honda. 'Maybe I could've made second on the last lap, but after Donington I had very much fear of crashing

again.' The weekend at the tortuous new Sachsenring wasn't entirely wasted, however. 'I realised I was still having problems with slow corners on the 250. They're difficult because you need to go slow mid-corner, then lift the bike really quickly and give gas when you're on the fatter part of the rear tyre, like Doohan used to.' He was already laying the foundations for his drive to 500s.

But it only took a few weeks off to forget that hard-learned lesson. He spent the mid-season break largin' it in Tunisia with Reggiani, Melandri & Co. and returned to Brno rested and ready to race. This time he lasted just four corners before falling. 'It was possible I win but I made the mistake because the fight between me, Capirossi and Harada was too much. Everyone say again: 'Rossi was okay with the best 125 but now he has same 250 as other guys, it's another story'. After Brno I took all the negative power and transformed it into positive power. I don't know how, I think I just understood better, so I became a lot calmer. It was a very bad time, but I arrived at the next races harder and more focused.'

Just four races remained in which he might prove to everyone that he was more than just a fast fool; two in Europe – Imola and Catalunya – and two outside – Australia and Argentina. Valentino won the lot, pushing Capirossi into second on each occasion. And he did so in style, wearing a tricolor hairdo at Imola and, still unable to resist playing the clown, riding his Catalunya victory lap with a chicken on the pillion. Well, a friend dressed up as a chicken. That jape got Valentino into

Matching Imola tricolore hairdo only made the swooning Valenteeny-boppers swoon some more. (Gold & Goose)

His first home-race special paintjob worked wonders, a runaway win at Imola '98 which began a season-ending run of four victories. (Gold & Goose)

A new alter ego for '99. 'We needed a superhero to come back from the bad situation of '98, so Valentino became a superhero and became Valentinik!' (Gold & Goose)

conflict with series organisers Dorna, who were growing increasingly tired of the boy's displays, which might interfere with their precious race schedule and encourage fans to invade the racetrack. He was unrepentant: 'I'll do the same thing again because I like to amuse the fans. I think the GP bosses want to make motorcycle racing like F1 and I don't think that's right. I don't like F1 because it seems everyone is only there for the money, while bikes are about passion.'

The final win at Buenos Aires was achieved in blissful ignorance of a title-deciding contretemps between Capirossi and Harada. Harada had been running second at the last-but-one turn, good enough for the title, when Capi arrived at warp-factor five, wiping out the Japanese rider to claim the crown for himself. That left Valentino just shy of winning the championship, too close for comfort: 'I lose the title by just three points, shit!'

Looking back at his first 250 season, he had done a lot of growing up, he was no longer the naive teenager merely out for some fun. 'That summer changed me in life and as a rider, it was a bad period but maybe necessary. I very much change my comportment in the paddock, when I am with people who are not my friends. I become more clever and less impulsive, so when I speak with journalists I stay more quiet, because it's like the police: "What you say may be used against you". But when I am Valentino, in my mind and with my friends, I maybe became less serious, maybe have more fun, because it's necessary.'

During 1998 racing also ceased to be playtime and his 250 rivals weren't playmates. 'In 125s everyone is like a family, everyone stays friends, it's not like that in 250s,' he said halfway through the year. 'I don't like the way some 250 riders behave. Before I came into 250s a lot of them were my heroes, but not any more. Some guys like Ukawa get in my way and try and slow me down when I'm on a fast qualifying lap. Then they say they didn't see me, but for sure they did, no one ever did that when I was in 125s.'

No worries; he'd teach them. He knew he didn't need to change much for 1999, just his alter ego: out with Rossifumi, in with Valentinik. 'We needed a super-hero to come back from the bad situation of '98. We were preparing to win in '99, so we chose a superhero

based on Italian comic hero Paparinik. Paparino is Donald Duck in Italian and Walt Disney has a duck superhero called Paparinik, who wears a mask and a cape, but he's not like Superman, he's a little bit unlucky, he makes some mistakes, some casino, but at the end of every story he's always the superhero. Paparino becomes a superhero and becomes Paparinik, so Valentino became a superhero and became Valentinik!' Simple, really…

And the 1999 world title could hardly have looked easier. Vale was now solo numero uno at Aprilia, Harada having graduated to the factory's 500 twin, Capirossi back at Honda after getting the flick for his Buenos Aires indiscretion. But if HRC had squeezed more speed from their NSR, the bike was still slower than the Aprilia, although marginally faster than the sluggish but sweet-handling YZRs of Yamaha's new challengers Olivier Jacque and Shinya Nakano.

The 16-race campaign began true to the Valentinik script: bike trouble at Malaysia's new space-age venue Sepang and a dismal seventh in pouring rain at Honda's grim new Motegi circuit; 'I still don't like riding under the water,' he explained.

Back to Europe, already a worrying 21 points down on joint series leaders Capirossi and Nakano. Time for another miracle renaissance. 'But this was different from '98, I was in a deeper hole in '98, this time I arrive at Jerez relaxed and, no problem, I win.' He coolly defeated Ukawa's NSR, Nakano retiring with bike trouble, and celebrated in hilarious fashion, dumping

his RSW on its side and diving into a trackside Portaloo.

'On the Thursday I was jogging around the track with Uccio and we saw this toilet. I thought: 'Why they have just one toilet out here, all alone?' So I say: "For sure, if I win I go in." When he reappeared, the crowd went berserk.

Two weeks later it was Valentino's turn to suffer bike trouble. Cruising to an easy win at Ricard his Aprilia's drive chain jumped the sprockets, leaving him languishing trackside and fourth on points, 40 down on race winner Ukawa. Now there was a mountain to climb. 'I found myself in a strange situation. I was fighting for the title with Ukawa and though I knew I was faster, I knew I couldn't afford one mistake because the gap would increase to 60 points and I'd be facked. I always knew in my mind that I could beat Ukawa, but if he kept finishing second it'd take eight races just to catch him. So I stay quiet and relaxed.'

From here on in, he rode the knife edge like a master. He won eight of the last 12 races, finished second twice and third once, only missing the podium at rainy Valencia, still struggling with that water stuff. Poor Ukawa didn't know what had hit him.

The rout had begun on home tarmac at Mugello, Valentino's special home-race leathers and bodywork resplendent in swirly Seventies-style graphics, proclaiming 'Valentinipeace&love'. Aprilia Germany's Ralf Waldmann came in second at a respectful distance, Ukawa third. The race had been a walk in the

Who's the funny guy? Vale interrupts his Jerez victory lap for possibly his best-ever post-race jape. (Gold & Goose)

REPSOL
Fuel & Oils

REPSOL
Fuel & Oils

park, the victory lap less so. Valentino ended up submerged beneath an ecstatic Latin throng killing him with their kindness. 'I was trying to escape the crowd, then I run into a cameraman and fall down. The Italians went crazy, it was a nightmare, I think I would die.'

Two weeks later at Catalunya, another win and fastest lap, Ukawa yapping at his heels all the way, but well covered at every turn. The next Saturday at Assen he looked very ragged, very unRossi, as Capirossi wreaked revenge, beating him by a fraction, with Ukawa, Nakano and Briton Jeremy McWilliams right in there too. 'Assen wasn't a race, it was a battle. That sometimes happens, you stop with the right lines and just fight, like remove one chip from your brain and put in another. It was me against Capirossi, and, fack, I lost.'

At least he'd got something of a buzz in qualifying, bettering Biaggi's previously unbeaten 1995 pole record. 'The Aprilia mechanics who worked with Biaggi

in '95 were working on Harada's 500 in '99, and they kept telling me I'd never beat that lap. After the final session I couldn't resist going into their pit and having a little laugh at them!' The achievement mattered all the more because Assen is considered GP racing's ultimate test of rider talent. 'It's like a horizontal rollercoaster,' said Valentino, already wondering what it might be like on a 500. 'No problem on a 125, a little problem on a 250 and maybe a very big problem on a 500. Watching the 500s there is scary, they're so fast and wobbling all over!'

During July he paid back Capirossi, beating him by a fraction at Donington and Sachsenring, and all of a sudden he was leading the championship. If anyone had previously doubted the depth and breadth of the boy's talent, there could be but one or two doubters left, and Honda certainly wasn't one of them. The world's biggest bike brand wanted in on the Rossi

phenomenon, Honda Italy and Doohan initiating a scramble that gained momentum until there was a hint of the rampant about it. Honda weren't going to take no for an answer. Hell, there hadn't been a bike star like this – so talented, so saleable – in decades. At first he played hard to get: 'I'm in no hurry, I'm not obsessed with doing 500s, I have a good relationship with Aprilia and I see no reason to leave.'

There wasn't just one offer from Honda either, there were two, one from Honda Europe and one from Doohan, who was planning to create his own team after suffering career-ending injuries at Jerez in May 1999. At Brno, where he won again to secure the first of two 250 hat-tricks, he was still thinking Aprilia. And by Imola he was already getting sick of people quizzing him about his plans.

If these were confusing times for Valentino, they must've been an absolute whirl for his hairdresser. At

Donington in July he'd gone a hair colour too far: green, which followed less criminal cranial outbursts of orange, grey, blue, blond, black/blond and red/green/blond. Presumably realising the error of his ways, he quickly had the greened locks shaved off and then had his skinhead neatly adapted for Imola to replicate Brazzi's naked pate. Brazzi was touched by this grinning gesture of respect: 'It was typical of Valentino's nature, his way of joking with his people, his way of showing his appreciation.' Didn't work though. Valentino succumbed to Capirossi's Honda once again, his over-stiff and unstable Aprilia lacking traction out of the slower turns. Luck was on his side once again, however, because closest points-challenger Ukawa limped in 12th after a mid-race tumble.

The next day he was holed up in an Imola hotel room, holding the first of many secret meetings with HRC personnel. 'They wanted me to say yes or no immediately,

but I said: "Sorry, I want to win 250 before I make decision". The hard thing for me was leaving Brazzi's team because they'd become like family to me. But I told Brazzi then, "If I win title, my work in 250 is finished".'

After an eighth-place finish at rainy Valencia the circus headed out of Europe for the last four races, Valentino pursued everywhere he went by Honda representatives and an ever-growing pack of spying Italian journalists, gathered here and there in conspiratorial huddles. At windswept Phillip Island he somehow managed to keep his head in the midst of the feeding frenzy, recovering from a bruising crash in qualifying to win a classic four-way battle with Jacque, Ukawa and Nakano. 'During practice we didn't have so much rear grip and eventually we realised it was a gearbox problem; the gearing was too tall so I wasn't able to transfer weight to the rear tyre when I was getting on the gas. My mechanics lowered the gearing on Saturday evening and that made the difference.'

While his crew toiled on his RSW he sneaked across the makeshift Phillip Island paddock – all Portakabins and corrugated sheds – to visit the HRC pit. Inside was Jerry Burgess, Doohan's crew chief who'd been twiddling his thumbs ever since the Aussie's bone-crunching crash at Jerez. Burgess was the man who would be looking after Valentino if he did make the switch and this was their first meeting.

'It was like when I first met Mick way back in '88; the important thing was to listen and to understand what he would want from us if he were to join Honda,' recalls JB. 'Then I showed him over the NSR500 and he listened to everything, took it all on board, even though I wasn't doing a salesman deal on him because he wanted a Honda, he knew it was the bike to do the job in 500s. He was very quiet, which I always think is a great sign of intelligence. I pretty much said to him that if he got to the top of Honda's pyramid of riders, we'd do whatever he wanted to make things work.'

Mugello '99: peace and love to everyone, except anyone who happened to be sharing the racetrack with him. (Gold & Goose)

The Mugello race was easy, the victory lap less so. Moments later he tumbled from his Aprilia... (Gold & Goose)

...and was swamped by a suffocating crowd of fans and well wishers. 'I think I would die.' (Gold & Goose)

One close look at Honda's money-no-object NSR was enough to make up Valentino's mind. 'When I see the bike up close I say: "This is the bike, maybe it's necessary we go to 500".'

Directly from Melbourne to South Africa, for the first GP at the brand-new and only just completed Welkom venue outside a gold-mining town fallen on hard times. Once again, Valentino and his crew battled set-up problems. 'We always struggled at slippery, bumpy circuits because the Aprilia has such a stiff chassis', but he won anyway. By now there was a sense of the relentless about the racing; after a messy start he casually brushed aside all opposition to head home Nakano's easier-handling YZR. If things kept going like this he'd clinch the title at Rio in a fortnight.

The Italian media could barely contain themselves, their hysteria tweaked more by rumours that he was defecting to Honda than by his genius stroll to the title. He found the fuss hilarious: 'They make a big casino because I will be racing against Biaggi for the first time. For sure Biaggi will be difficult to beat, especially in my first year. He's one of the best 500 riders, but at the end of the day he's only another rider.' The papers could see exactly what was coming.

At Rio he came back from another sluggish getaway to hunt down Capirossi, Ukawa, and Jacque, then saunter past to take his ninth win and collect the crown. Not only that, he also became the youngest 250 world champ, taking the record away from the late Mike Hailwood who'd been 21 when he won the title in 1961. Valentino had flown 20 members of his fan club to Brazil for the occasion and celebrated with a riotous party at a nearby yacht club, where he was tossed fully dressed into the swimming pool. That same evening he made another clandestine visit to a hotel room, where he met the men from HRC once again. 'I say to the Japanese: "Okay, we are ready".'

Aprilia still had a bigger pile of cash on the table, their deal reputedly worth £2.3 million, although he refuses to talk numbers. 'I always knew Honda would be less money but at that point in my career I never think about money because it's necessary to concentrate on racing.' Although the fine details were thrashed out at a later date, Valentino was destined to be his own one-man team, outside of the Repsol Honda clique, which allowed him to run his own sponsors, his own livery and his own favourite colour. 'When I make this kind of decision I try to go the way that gives me the most freedom. So with Nastro Azzurro and my other sponsors I can make a yellow bike. Yellow is my colour, like 46 is my number.'

It was back to business the following Sunday for the season finale in Argentina, where an incorrect tyre choice left him third behind Jacque and Ukawa. Or maybe his mind had been on other things: Aprilia had generously granted him an early release from his contract, so HRC had booked Jerez for his first 500 test just four weeks hence. Okay, he could ride a 250 but…

If imitation is the sincerest form of flattery…Imola skinhead faithfully mimicked engineer Brazzi's balding cranium. (Henk Keulemans)

Celebrating the title at Rio '99. There are those who suspect that Valentino always rides with angels. (Gold & Goose)

Vale was transformed from boy to man during his two 500 seasons, the zany post-race parades replaced by gloriously executed rolling burn-outs. (Gold & Goose)

a poet
in motion

All the racetrack and a little bit more, that's always been Valentino's style. His signature is the flurry of dirt kicked up from trackside as he carves an extravagantly wide line in search of the fastest launch out of a corner. It's a perilous technique, especially on a viciously overpowered motorcycle like an NSR500. It's tempting fate, then giving fate the finger, and that's exactly why he likes doing it. Plus, of course, going that extra centimetre is a key element in his ability to magic the best out of a racetrack.

'I always like to go to the edge, because it give me a power. If I can exit a corner for ten laps every time one centimetre from the edge of the track, I feel everything is under control. I've always had a big passion for the line, for me the line is like a poem. My focus is always for my lines to be within the same centimetre every time for 20 laps. This feels good, because you can do one fast lap all with your heart, with the eyes shut, but it's not easy to ride 20 laps like that. Sometimes I crash because of my passion for the line. Uccio and Gibo say 'Fack, stay 50 centimetres inside', but it's my passion.'

Sito Pons Corner, Jerez, December 1999. Valentino is riding out of the circuit's most important turn, a blind 85mph right-hander that crosses the brow of a hill, then plunges the rider down into the track's fastest straight. He is looking stiffer than usual, a little hesitant, nothing like he had looked 30 days earlier in South America where he'd been master of a 96hp motorcycle. Now, here he was a few weeks later, a 190 horse motorcycle very much his master. He's exiting the

corner, the revs building fast, then too fast as the rear slick loses traction and smears sideways, driving the motorcycle off the tarmac and across the kerb where he fights a mother of a tankslapper. He stays on but it's hardly poetry in motion.

'Valentino looked a little awkward on the bike initially, I mean it's a big step,' says crew chief Jerry Burgess who has vivid memories of that first test with Alex Criville's title-winning NSR. 'I wouldn't say he was awestruck, he gave the impression that he was pretty much prepared for anything, but he was feeling his way that first time, he knew he had some learning to do.'

If anyone was awestruck, it was Burgess and his ex-Doohan crew: Bernard Ansiau, Alex Briggs, Dickie Smart and Gary Coleman. After years of sweating in the pressure-cooker of Mick's pit box they could hardly believe the aura of calm in which they found themselves. Burgess: 'The guys were like: "Jesus, isn't he great?" and I was saying: "Yeah, I know, it's fantastic". We had to do a complete mind switch because we'd gone from working for the grandfather, and thinking like that, to getting on with the mentality of a 21-year-old. For me, approaching 50, that was very enlightening and part of it was getting some enjoyment out of the way Valentino sees life.'

Pretty soon the guys discovered that Valentino wasn't just fun to work with, he also had real intelligence, an enquiring and analytical mind that would allow him to quickly convince any doubters that he really is one of the all-time greats, not just a great 125 and 250 rider. After a predictably shaky start, while he attempted to locate the 500's limit, he swiftly rose up to conquer his NSR and then the entire 500 grid. The group of riders who had been elevated to the status of title fighters by Doohan's crunching exit from racing only enjoyed the briefest moment of glory before Valentino had them done and dusted. His 13 500 GP victories from the next two seasons exceed even Doohan's win rate; 40.6 per cent to 39.4 per cent.

After Jerez, Burgess's first job was to revise the NSR's riding position for its gangly new pilot, then get down to the task of adapting every facet of machine performance to suit his riding style. 'From the start Valentino was very open about any problems he was having with the 500,' he says. 'And when we made modifications he was very open about whether they were an improvement or not. We quickly learned that he's very good at working on set-up. When he comes into the pits he's like a computer. He gives you a list of six or eight things he wants looking at, like a download. He's more analytical than the rest of them. I think we have a lot to thank his parents for because they gave us a kid who can think logically and also Aprilia, who gave him the training so he can say what the problem is and whether we're making the bike better or worse. But back at the start we could see that he was looking forward more to the racing.'

There was much to learn before the season started, although things were looking pretty rosy. After all, he'd just joined the factory that had won every 500 riders' and manufacturers' title since 1994, so there was no doubt he'd got his hands on the best 500. No doubt, at least, until the 2000 season actually started, when it quickly became apparent that something had gone very, very wrong with the NSR. This was the year that Honda lost the riders' crown to Suzuki's Kenny Roberts and its manufacturers' title to Yamaha.

The reasons for the upheaval in factory fortunes were several. Suzuki and Yamaha were trying harder than ever, and their riders, especially Roberts and Marlboro Yamaha's Max Biaggi, were coming nicely to the boil. Also, Doohan was no longer around at HRC, which put Criville top of the pyramid. Without the Aussie's guiding light HRC were lost in the darkness, the engineers making the mistake of listening to a

rider, well, listening to a rider who didn't really know what he wanted.

'It's like Honda did with Wayne Gardner when he won the title in '87,' explains Burgess, who had guided the rodeo-riding Aussie to the 500 crown after working with triple world champ Freddie Spencer. 'They asked what Wayne wanted and he asked for more power. That's what Alex asked for too. More power is easy enough, so long as you can open the throttle, but the new engine was very different in terms of power delivery. Later on an HRC engineer told me that Mick wouldn't have done half a lap with the 2000 engine, so I asked the guy: "Why the hell would you make it then?", but it was what Alex wanted. Alex didn't have the experience, he'd always just followed along in Mick's slipstream, beating him from time to time when things went his way.'

Incredibly Valentino clocked the dodgy power delivery the very first time he rode the new NSR at Phillip Island in early 2000. It took HRC's more experienced men longer to realise they'd got a serious problem. 'All the power had been moved to the top, so there was nothing there when you were fully leaned over in the middle of the corner, so you'd give it some more throttle and there'd be too much power,' Burgess explains. 'He said it felt too neutral in the middle of the corners.' Which is how Valentino crashed on that first outing.

No worries; by round one at Welkom he was well up to speed, qualifying just a tenth of a second off the front row. He also set the fastest lap of the race, moments before he crashed out, losing his NSR right in the middle of a turn, like it just rolled over and died. Aussie terrier of slide Garry McCoy won the race, Carlos Checa second on a Yamaha, and Loris Capirossi third on a '99 NSR. Same deal at round two; Valentino low-level flying into a heap again, this time Roberts the winner ahead of Checa and McCoy. The factory Hondas were nowhere once more and within HRC the accusations began to fly.

Burgess could see from the computer readouts why Valentino was crashing and why the other NSR riders were struggling, but was unable to do much about it via HRC. 'Valentino was the new boy on the block, fourth in the pecking order behind the Repsol guys:

'And this here is the clutch.' Jerry Burgess introduces Valentino to the NSR500, Jerez, December 1999. (Gold & Goose)

Alex, Tady (Okada) and Sete (Gibernau). Plus he'd got no points on the board so we couldn't go in there screaming and shouting.'

Yet despite Valentino's deadly unimpressive start, HRC didn't take long to realise they had hired themselves an exceptional talent. While the media were already wondering if he'd got what it takes to cut it in 500s, HRC had some definitive evidence suggesting that he surely would. His data traces didn't only highlight the NSR's problems, they also showed that Valentino already had more refined throttle control, the essential weapon in a 500 rider's armoury, than other HRC riders like Criville, veteran of more than a hundred 500 starts.

HRC was also impressed with Valentino's fighting spirit. 'He was carving through the pack at Welkom and Sepang, trying to do what he thought he could do,'

recalls Burgess. 'So they'd seen that he had the determination to get the bike to the front and this is what's very much rewarded at Honda. Anyone who just rides around doesn't get a lot of say, but there's always hope for the guy who pushes hard, even if he falls down, it's like: "We can work with this guy".'

Valentino didn't know that at the time and the two crashes had rattled his cage. He arrived at Suzuka for round three physically and psychologically bruised, and it showed on the track: 13th on the grid, 11th in the race, his worst result since his earliest 125 GP days. Perhaps this really was a class too far. 'Valentino was very, very badly spooked by the two non-finishes and he was very spooked by the 11th place. Suzuka was a complete shutdown of a guy who could've done better.'

After Japan the circus returned to Europe. Would

Valentino get it together on more familiar tarmac, or, having started digging himself a hole, would he continue to dig? The comeback at round four in Spain was as emphatic as those he'd managed in 125 and 250: first front-row 500 start and first podium behind Roberts and Checa. New engines parts, or rather old '99 parts, had arrived for Jerez and Valentino was back on a bike that he could work with.

'Once we got to Europe we started to kick off,' says Burgess who had quickly established an excellent working relationship with his new charge. 'You didn't have to be Einstein to work out what he was capable of. The talent was obviously there for anyone to see, so long as he was kept happy and kept in the right frame of mind. So I was emphatic with the team and everyone around us, I told them that this guy isn't going to fail unless we fail him and the only way we can fail him is if he's not happy within this team network. So the number one priority is to keep him happy.'

Racing is all in the mind, so Burgess's job is to ooze confidence, to instill his rider with the belief that he really can go that extra two tenths faster. 'In this game it's 80 per cent in the rider's head and 20 per cent in the machine,' he says. 'So if your rider wants gold handlebars, you give him gold handlebars.' Or you do if he knows what he's talking about and Burgess had already sussed that Valentino knows exactly what he was talking about. 'There are some riders who don't know what they want, they ask for stuff simply out of the frustration of not obtaining decent lap times; so

you could move the geometry all around and then nobody knows what's going on. The old KISS principle doesn't work too badly on a motorcycle: keep it simple, stupid.' Burgess is an arch-pragmatist. While some rival engineers vainly attempt to reinvent the wheel to give their rider an advantage, he stays firmly grounded in the realms of the possible, his fundamental attitude to his job summed up by his father's racing principle, the five Ps: perfect preparation prevents poor performance.

But Valentino's astounding gift for understanding and analysing machine performance was about to show Burgess that the realms of the possible could be expanded. At Le Mans, all second-gear hairpins, he spirited himself through the pack after a so-so start, setting a new lap record as he caught leaders Roberts, Criville and Yamaha's Norick Abe. This was his first time properly up front and his first real opportunity to compare himself to his rivals and their machines. 'Valentino really started to talk about the bike after Le Mans. He said that where Alex had wheelspin, he also had wheelspin, but at that same point Abe's Yamaha would still be driving forward with traction. That's when we started the ball rolling for the NV4A, the derivative NSR which we used for the last few races of 2000, which developed into the NV4B he used in 2001.'

Two weeks later was the biggest day of his life: the Italian GP at Mugello and his first premier-class race on home tarmac. Whole hillsides tinged yellow by his fans, outbreaks of Biaggi red here and there. Valentino's shaky start was fast being forgotten by the media who

Maybe these 500s aren't so easy, after all. Valentino eats tarmac at Sepang, his second crash in as many races. (Gold & Goose)

were now salivating at the prospect of the first Rossi versus Biaggi duel. Whoever was writing the script was doing a great job: two Italian fighters set for a home-town brawl, no, make that three, Capirossi was up there too. One nation, three gladiators.

Qualifying was super close, the trio split by 0.132 seconds: Biaggi second, Rossi third, Capirossi fourth, Alex Barros on pole. The race was even closer, the trio trading blows out front, no doubt about it, this was going to end in tears. One and a half laps to go and Valentino hit the attack button, slid into the lead, then lost the front and fell at the next turn. Doohan, recently appointed HRC general manager to keep an eye on Honda's young chargers, had seen it all coming: 'He started riding the bike like a 250, running pretty deep into corners, he just got in there too hot and loaded up the front.'

Biaggi lasted another lap before colliding with Capirossi and falling, leaving Capirex to cruise across the line. Burgess had found the entire weekend an enlightening experience. 'I was unaware of what the Max/Valentino thing was about, I pretty much thought it was a media thing. I didn't know that Italy only became a country in 1871, so a lot of the regions still don't like each other.' Too right, it's Italy's north–south divide, the mezzogiorno, one of the reasons the pair are apparently irreconcilable. Biaggi is Roman, he's old-school Italian, resides in Monaco and has tea with the Pope; Valentino is from the Marches region, he's new-skool Italian, hangs out in London and goes clubbing with his mates.

So their first clash had ended nil-all; it wouldn't be their last. From now on every time they were in the same room together, usually only when duty called for pre- and post-race press conferences, the air crackled with animosity. Words would not be spoken, their eyes would never meet, and yet somehow they managed to keep a lid on it for another year.

At Catalunya Valentino rode his first wet 500 race, easing home third like he'd been doing it all his life, and remember this was the man who hated riding 'under the water'. Thirteen years earlier three-time 500 champ Wayne Rainey had ridden his first wet 500 GP, watched by his father. Sandy was awestruck, petrified

by these meanest of machines, 'these things that don't even want you on their backs,' as he called them. True, rain tyres and digitally controlled power curves had come a long way since '88 and Catalunya's designer turns aren't the cold-steel lined sweepers of Spa, but this was another moment that history seemed to whisper his name. While all around people were losing their heads – the race turned into something of a crash fest – Valentino kept his, gleefully juggling the throttle, twisting his NSR sideways out of the turns.

At Assen he came in sixth after threatening the leaders before the rain came down. Two weeks later at Donington, more rain, for this was the year that swollen grey clouds followed the circus everywhere. Using wets on a drying track, Valentino jostled with championship leader Roberts and Jeremy McWilliams, smokin' his overheating rear tyre as he launched out of turns to win by a fraction. His first 500 victory had hardly come as a surprise.

His next ride, to second at the Sachsenring, was even more impressive. He may have been learning the art of 500 riding with astounding speed but he still hadn't acquired the ability to launch a 190hp/130kg motorcycle from the grid, a delicate balancing act requiring immaculate throttle/clutch interaction. Too much throttle, too much clutch and it's loop-the-loop time, too little and you get wasted on the dash to turn one. Valentino got destroyed, 16th at the end of the first lap, and this at a tortuous track where it's reckoned there's little or no room for overtaking. So he made some, conjuring lines that others seemed incapable of using, making fools of 500 racing's great and good as he picked them off wherever he pleased. With five laps to go he was ahead, then he bungled the final lap, crossing the line eight hundredths behind Barros.

'I'm very used to coming from the back because I've never been a very good starter, it was the same in 125 and 250. Like at Barcelona 2001, I started from pole but was almost last at the first corner after I collide with someone. Maybe other riders would have thought "Oh fack, we're lost", but I did the same in 250 there in '99 and the same at Sachsenring in 2000, just stay calm and go. It's always been quite easy for me to overtake anywhere, but I don't think that's because I'm better than the other guys, just because I try. Many other riders say that it's very hard to overtake at the Sachsenring, okay so it is, but if you try, maybe it's not very hard.' If only it was that easy for everyone.

After Germany the little matter of the Suzuka Eight Hours. This classic event, acted out in Japan's high summer of withering 35° heat and 80 per cent humidity, is the most important event in the world to Honda because of its influence on the massive domestic bike market. The roll call of winners includes illustrious names like Doohan, Rainey, Gardner and Eddie Lawson, all of them former 500 kings. But most GP riders loathe the race, finding it an awkward distraction from the real job of winning the World Championship. Not only can the switch to unfamiliar four-stroke machinery affect their 500 riding, but the factories' obsession with winning the event demands their stars' presence at pre-event tests. Poor Valentino had to go to Japan not once but twice during the five weeks preceding the race, delivering two doses of strength-sapping jetlag. Then again, he had asked for it. While Doohan had spent years fighting to get the Eight Hours scrubbed from his HRC contract, Valentino had volunteered for the job. 'I always love Eight Hours from when I was young because I love the Japanese colours and graphics. When I was at Aprilia I push very hard with Jan Witteveen (Aprilia's technical chief) to race an RSV Mille there. Also I want to try a Superbike, I want to ride with Superbike riders, see their level.'

So here was another question: okay, so he could ride 125, 250 and 500 two-strokes but how would he cope with the very different demands of a four-stroke? This wasn't merely idle contemplation, there was a crucial significance to his Eight Hour performance because GP racing was awaiting a landmark shift in technical regulations. From 2002 the premier class would be going four-stroke.

Surprise, surprise, Valentino had little trouble adapting to the factory SP-1 Superbike he'd share with race partner Colin Edwards, who went on to win the 2001 World Supers crown. He found the softer, heavier SP-1 easy to ride and deceptively quick. 'The bike is incredible, it feels slow but the lap time is almost the same as with the NSR. You can ride the Superbike at

Now he's getting the hang of it, leading Roberts, Checa, Barros and Biaggi at Mugello. (Gold & Goose)

100 per cent all the time, is easy. With 500 you can ride it 100 per cent maybe three or four times a season, and when you use the 500 at 100 per cent, it's not like different class, it's like different sport.' Is easy but not that easy – Vale and his American team-mate led the race, then they had a crash each. Situation normal: new bike, necessary find limit.

Already GP racing's biggest star, he was downgraded to non-person for the next GP at Brno. Vale had left his passport at home, so he smuggled himself over the Czech border, competing as an illegal alien. Not that anyone seemed to notice, let alone care. Second there and third in Portugal he now found himself hauling in points leader Roberts. With three races to go he was 46 points behind the son of a legend, a long call but not impossible. Was he about to change the habit of a lifetime and win something at the first attempt?

It seemed unlikely, since he was happy to admit that he was still struggling to get the hang of riding a 500 and even more so the labyrinthine art of refining the bike's settings to suit his style. 'I still have problems understanding the 500, I still can't use 100 per cent of the bike,' he said in Portugal. What he really wanted was to ride a 500 like his childhood heroes, the 'Old Dogs' as he called them, brave men like Schwantz, Doohan, Rainey and Gardner who raced with reckless throttle hands, kicking out the bike's ass end and getting 'kinda squirrelly'. 'They were the true 500 riders and my dream is to use a 500 like those guys.'

He'd get there very soon but not just yet. His title charge ended in the gravel at Valencia after he'd teetered on the brink once too often, asking too much edge grip from the front tyre, still riding the thing like it was a 250. He effectively crashed twice in the race, except he somehow managed to save the first. This was Vale in rare rostrum-or-hospital mode. Burgess: 'He pretty much knew that if he didn't beat Roberts there then the title was gone. If he had beaten him there he could've kept the title open right to the last race, that was the way he saw it.'

Down in Rio he bounced back with his first dry-weather 500 win, dismissing Barros, McCoy, Abe and Biaggi with a new-found confidence – he'd finally managed to kick his 250 habits and start riding the NSR like a true 500 rider. 'In Rio we change my style very much because I basically crash two times at Valencia, the first, whooooa,' he says, doing a very passable imitation of his big sideways moment. 'The second I crash, so I speak with Jeremy (Vale is one of the few people who uses JB's full Christian name), we watch the race and understand I need to change my style because I make very much crash with the front tyre. Until this race I was quite fast but I ride like 250, so I always finish the front tyre after half the race.'

So Valentino adapted his cornering lines. He reduced the arc of corner entry, lowering his mid-corner speed and focusing all his efforts into a straight drive out of the turn. That way he could lay down as much horsepower as his rear Michelin would allow and a little bit more, using the wheelspin to get sideways, pointing his NSR's front end back towards the inside of the corner, tightening his line and giving him more room to get on the gas, which means more speed down the next straight. It's like using the handbrake in a car, except he breaks traction with the throttle, not the brake.

'The perfect line is stay wide, wide, wide and after you close the line and go in inside, slowing a little bit to the apex. With the 250 it's possible to do this and if you make like this with the 500 you are very fast but when you go to close the line after seven laps you lose the front and you crash. So necessary go inside a little bit early and a little bit more, use less speed in the corner and after pick up the bike and accelerate. So I change very much the first part of the corner. Not so much the second part because when I ride 250 I already ride a little bit like 500, picking up the bike to accelerate, more than other 250 riders. In Rio I use less speed in the corner and start to spin the rear tyre very much on the exit.

'For many years I train for spinning with motocross bike because sliding and spinning is also very much fun. But spinning was impossible with the 250 because not enough power, so when I arrive in 500 I want to try and I get better and better. In winter I still train on the dirt, using a motocross front tyre and trail-bike rear tyre with little grip, so I'm sideways all the time, this gives me a big help for sliding the 500.'

Like Donington there were no comedy post-race gags at Rio, just a loving hug for his NSR. By now they were the best of mates, and if investing an inanimate object with life sounds nuts, it isn't, it helps cement that man–machine bond so crucial in racing. During 2000 Vale flaunted their thriving relationship with the post-race rolling burn-out, a tricky stunt that became his favourite way of telling the world what a laugh he was having out there. 'The 250 never had enough power but it's sweet on the 500, you just spin the tyre till it gets hot and there's no grip, then you only need a little throttle. I like it very much.'

Onward to Motegi for the Pacific GP where he couldn't catch a runaway Roberts but did defeat Biaggi in a last-lap duel, their first serious encounter since Mugello. 'Passing him,' he said afterwards. 'Was like the best orgasm.' One-nil. But Biaggi had his revenge two weeks later, brave winner of an epic season-ending Australian GP, Capirossi second, Vale third, the three of them separated by just two tenths. He ended the championship second behind Roberts, although there was no doubt who'd been strongest in the later stages of the series. And if he hadn't crashed out of those first two races…

Winter was dedicated to perfecting the NV4A prototype he had raced for the first time at Valencia, refining the chassis, cylinders, ignition mapping and carburettors. This bike was tailor made for Valentino, according to his desire for improved rear-end traction, because now there was no doubt who was HRC's number one. 'It was the first time HRC had really changed the NSR's chassis since '91,' says Burgess. 'They were ecstatic they'd got a guy with new ideas.'

In between test sessions in Australia, Malaysia and Europe Vale got on with the rest of his life: snowboarding with mates, doing some rallying and moving to London. He rented a West-End apartment in the British capital because he needed to get out of Italy but couldn't handle the thought of moving to Monaco, the VIP ghetto that is home to so many GP riders, F1 drivers and other chinless tax exiles. 'I could live there for two days, but after that? Is not the real world.' London is the real world, urban mayhem and gridlock, so he blagged an SP-1 and a FireBlade from Honda UK, then settled on a less hectic CBR600. Most of all though he was having fun descending into London clubland with his mates who were taking it in turns flying over from Italy to help him party. In October he had split up with longtime girlfriend Eliane Ferni so he was out on the loose, often at the upmarket China White Club near Piccadilly which counts Prince Andrew amongst its other clientele. Oh well, you can't have everything.

At Valencia he teetered on the brink once too often, ending his slim hopes of winning the 500 crown at his first attempt. (Gold & Goose)

'For 500s you need to be quiet, calm and thoughtful; more like a doctor.' So, exit Valentinik, enter The Doctor. (Gold & Goose)

winning
very much

Pre-ride rituals are vital to racers. They provide an ordered system of preparation devoid of the unforeseen, so the rider can maintain his focus on his machine and retain all his mental capacity to deal with whatever mayhem might be unleashed on the racetrack. Like most racers, Valentino's pre-ride ritualism has little to do with superstition; how could any serious racer believe that the outcome of a race might depend on how he slips on his gloves? No, it's just a procedure that allows him to prepare as perfectly as possible for each outing. Through order comes calm, so his leathers and back protector are always laid out in the same neat arrangement in the team truck and his helmet and gloves are always to be found in the same place in the pits. It's the only sure-fire way of avoiding the kind of 'Where the fack are my gloves?' nonsense

that might distract his mind or threaten his cool at such a vital moment.

His pre-ride routine is renowned, the TV cameras apparently endlessly fascinated by the process, which goes something like this: wet his fingers, massage eyes, fiddle with earring, pull on helmet, slip on gloves, walk towards bike, bend forward, squat down, grasp right footpeg – apparently performing some kind of communion with the motorcycle – climb aboard, tug bum of leathers while riding down pit-lane.

'When I make like this,' he smiles, grabbing the crotch of his jeans. 'Is only to make sure my leather are in the right position, is not superstition, if you want perfect leather for riding they're too baggy before you ride. Is the same with the squat, just to stretch the leather. The eye massage is because it's better for

He who dares wins. Vale uses all the track and a little more on his way to a historic victory at Suzuka 2001, Honda's 500th GP win. (Gold & Goose)

For once not looking in opposite directions, Valentino and Biaggi face the media as their 2001 title fight hots up. (Gold & Goose)

Just making sure he's comfortable. Valentino does his bum tug ritual as he rides out for qualifying. (Gold & Goose)

looking and I always touch my earring because, well, now is impossible to stop, is habit. For sure this also is not only superstition. If I know exactly where my things are it gives me a feeling of calm and security, so I can think only about the bike. At races I always arrive in the pit at the last moment, so if all is okay the time is enough, but if not I need more time and for sure I'm late to ride. I'm like this also when I'm away from the races, when possible I stay very organised.'

The regularity extends to Valentino's working days – Fridays, Saturdays and Sundays. 'Every day is the same. I go to bed around one and wake up eight-thirty, make the shower and make the breakfast: tea, biscuit and coffee. Then go to the pits, go in the team truck where I have my leather and everything and always music. The truck is office, the motorhome is home and always full because there's always someone staying. First practice and also race warm-up begin at ten and after I speak with my mechanics and eat at noon, then go to make massage at the Clinica Mobile

where they put Chinese deep-heat tape on my arms to make my muscles work better and to stop pump-up. Qualifying and race is at two and after I speak to Jeremy and have interview with all the journalists. When all is finished after practice I rest in my motorhome for one hour, listen to music, use my Playstation, then go and eat. After that I usually make sticker for my bike. When I was young I did all the stickers on my bikes, now I just do The Doctor, number 46, my own sticker. Then maybe spend the evening talking with friends about… nothing!'

Burgess has seen it all before: 'Valentino's method of operation is the same all the time, just like any professional sportsman's should be. Mick used to do it, he used to spend minutes and minutes putting his gloves on. It was a concentration thing, leaving one world behind and preparing to enter another. A racer ambles around the paddock at a few kays, then he's doing speeds of 300kmh, so he's got to have his wits around him. All the ritual stuff is like a buffer zone

'The way you see things, your view of the world, changes between the ages of 18 and 22'. Valentino proves he has a serious side. (Henk Keulemans)

between those two worlds, it puts the rider's mind in gear before he gets on the bike.'

Valentino's post-ride ritual is just as crucial to his race-day performance. He keeps to a strict debrief regime with JB and his crew. 'After practice we sit in the pits for ten minutes and he'll go through what happened in that session,' says Burgess. 'Then he'll talk to Juan (Martinez, Showa suspension technician) and me, making a lap on a circuit map, telling us what's happening with the bike. During that first conversation I'll ask him if we'll be changing the gearbox or anything else major, so we can do a certain amount of work before he comes back at six-ish when he talks with Juan and myself again, and within 20 minutes we've got it all done.

'Valentino uses his head, he thinks and he thinks and he thinks. He was great from the moment he started working with us at the end of '99, but there was a big change in him from 2000 to 2001, like he was coming out of being a teenager and becoming a man. In 2000 everything had been pretty spontaneous, in 2001 things were more methodical and thought out, more of the brain side coming in. I get the feeling he now feels he's an adult in an adult's world, while the previous five years of his career had just been good fun.'

Valentino agrees that his attitude to life has changed over the past few years. 'The way you see things, your view of the world, changes between the ages of 18 and 22,' he says. 'I'm older now, so I think I understand more, and for sure my life has changed. When you're 16 or 17 you don't have problems, unless it's something really big like family problems. Life is different when you're young, you only think about having fun.'

Riding the 500 changed him too, from boy to man. The daft victory celebrations faded into memory as a new-found seriousness took hold. He was growing up anyway and there was no way he could remain unaffected by the pressures of competing in racing's biggest class on the scariest race bikes known to man. 'The jokes also stop because I don't think a lot of people really understood the whole thing. It's like Mugello 2001 when we had my bikes painted Hawaii

The Doctor and
the Roman
Emperor prepare
to sort out their
differences at
Catalunya, first
on the track, then
in their infamous
post-race brawl.
(Gold & Goose)

style. When I crashed people said I only crashed because I'd been up all night painting them! So I decided it was better to stop all this and just wave like other riders, then have a big party on Sunday night with my real friends.' Plus he had new responsibilities helping Honda develop two amazing motorcycles, the last-of-the-line NSR500 and the RC211V, HRC's V5 weapon for the new four-stroke MotoGP class.

All this was reflected by a change in alter ego for 2001: exit Paparinik, enter The Doctor. 'We change because with 500s you don't need a superhero, you just need to be quiet, calm and thoughtful, more like a doctor,' he explains. 'Also, because in Italy there are very many doctors called Dr Rossi, so I became Dr Rossi.' The new nickname could hardly have been more apt, because he began 2001 in immaculate style, winning the first three races with surgical precision.

The season began at Suzuka, the circuit that Soichiro Honda built in 1962, where success means so much to the world's biggest bike brand. And this time more than ever. Honda had won a total of 497 world championship races since their first GP win in 1961, so a full house of 125, 250 and 500 victories at Suzuka would give them their 500th success. But it had been well over a year since they had won all three races in one day, so it seemed an impossible dream that Honda would attain the magic number on cherished home

tarmac. Especially since their 125s were well off the pace in qualifying.

'It was a Honda fantasy that they win their 500th race on that day,' Vale recalls. 'It was incredible, we watched the other races on TV and I say: 'For sure Honda won't win 125,' but fack, Azuma wins, then in 250 Kato wins, so fack, I must win 500.' And win he did, recovering from a scary 120mph collision with Biaggi to beat McCoy by less than a second and trigger massive celebrations within Honda. The Midas touch once again.

This was another of those days that had one idly wondering if the boy is perhaps blessed or if there's wizardry afoot in his life. Valentino's career was apparently evolving into an implausible plot for a cheesy Hollywood racetrack drama, *Days of Thunder* style. Anyone could have won Honda's 500th Grand Prix victory and it could have happened in any class at any track, but it didn't, it was Rossi, in the premier 500 class and at Suzuka.

The suggestion that greater forces might be at work in his life would keep returning throughout the next 12 months or so, not that they'd been entirely absent in previous years. At Donington in July he suffered a massive 125mph get-off during practice and walked away to win the race. Three years earlier the same corner had almost claimed Checa's life. During August's

Czech GP at Brno a bee flew inside his helmet, flew out again and he rode on to win the race. British 500 rider Leon Haslam suffered the same fate that weekend with very different consequences; he got stung and went blind in one eye, forcing him into the pits. By the end of the season Valentino had also won the closest 500 GP in history, at Phillip Island, and the final race of the 500 era at Rio, where a conveniently placed backmarker helped him beat Checa at the very last turn. Then he began the new age of four-strokes with victory at the 2002 Japanese GP, making it look too easy on a flooded Suzuka track, like he was walking on water. And to think, his father looks like Jesus …

Of course, you can attribute much of Valentino's success and apparent luck to his genius, but there's little doubt that he seems to enjoy more than his fair share of historical coincidences and lucky escapes. Some people are just like that, when things go right, they keep going right. Or as Eddie Lawson once said: 'The more I practise, the luckier I get'.

Wins at Welkom and Jerez completed the hat trick and these were dominant victories achieved at a dizzying speed, race records smashed at every track. Valentino was forcing the 500 pace for the first time since Doohan had disappeared, helped along by a new generation of Michelin slicks. He had quickly realised that the French company's 16.5-inch rear tyre offered

much better grip at the end of races, so he made the effort to adapt his settings to suit the tyre's different profile, while some of his rivals stuck with the easier-handling 17-inch tyre and paid the price at the end of races. Once again he was proving himself to be receptive to new ideas, all he wanted was speed, it didn't much matter what the bike felt like. 'After Mick stopped the 500 pace was always slow. I hated that, so it was time to raise the pace.'

And there were few that could run with him: Capirossi a lone and firmly defeated rival at Welkom, and no one to play with at Jerez after he'd finished toying with Abe. Valentino, like Doohan before him, was going quicker and quicker, the pack scattered behind him, and for a while it looked like 500 racing might return to those oh-so predictable Doohan days, when everyone awoke on Sundays with just one question on their minds: who'll get second?

Doohan, a hard man to impress but mellowing in retirement, was moved to fulsome praise by his protégé's lightning form. 'He's riding the bike like it should be ridden and he doesn't feel there's any reward in just running around with the pack. Some of the other guys have been caught out a little and guys like Max need to learn to ride the bike when it's not 100 per cent. When everything's good, Max is quick but when things aren't right…'

Valentino's yellow
army makes some
noise on the
hillsides around
Mugello...
(Gold & Goose)

...Max's red
brigade returns
fire from the
other side.
(Gold & Goose)

At Le Mans things did come right for Biaggi and he inflicted a major defeat on Valentino, who was pushed into third by Checa but still managed to tip his deadly rival a contemptuous wink on the podium. Cheeky. This was the start of Biaggi's tilt at the title. The Roman's technicians had made a crucial forward jump with machine settings, and when Valentino crashed out of the rain-lashed Italian GP, his arch-rival took another chunk out of his points lead. In the space of three races his advantage over Biaggi had shrunk from 46 to 21 points and tension was building. At Catalunya it exploded, the pair going for each others' throats in a cramped ante room after the race, which Vale had won in masterful style, recovering from a disastrous start to pick off his rivals and leave them trailing, Capirossi second, Biaggi third. The punch up between these two pumped up racers had been brewing for years, though it was more of an unseemly brawl than a man-to-man duel. There is no impartial record of exactly what happened because the pair were out of view when the fight kicked off, on their way to the post-race TV interview room with their various hangers-on.

'What happened wasn't very big and it wasn't important,' insists Valentino. 'It was like being at school: "He started it!" "No, he started it!" "No, he started it!". Biaggi said that I started this facking shit but it's necessary to think about what happened before. I started the race from last position and I arrived first at the flag, I made the fastest lap and I made a fantastic victory, so why would I want to make all that shit?'

According to one witness, Biaggi did manage to headbutt Valentino's team manager Carlo Fiorani while his arms were behind his back. Then he managed to fight free, clocking his nemesis in the face. If you were looking for a points decision in the absence of a knockout you'd probably give the fight to Mighty Max who won more cred in the post-race press conference when quizzed about his grazed face. 'A mosquito bit me,' he replied. The incident uncovered a streak of dignity within the older Italian, who was quick to remind everyone that he'd never stoked the fires of the long-running feud. 'My only defence is to say nothing,' he said, well aware of the difficulties of a PR offensive against everyone's favourite GP racer. All he did say was that Valentino only whacked him while Fiorani had his arms behind his back: 'That wasn't nice, it was unfair.'

Biaggi insists he's baffled by the rivalry. 'We only started racing together in 2000 but it feels like Rossi's been racing me ever since he was in 125s. It's not normal to have a go at another rider when you're not even in the same class. Rossi is clever, he gets energy from all this, but I think people get tired of it.' Of course, people weren't getting tired of it. This was more fun than anyone had had for years: a real, genuine confrontation between two riders who hate each other's guts. Somehow it makes the racing more real, more urgent.

A somewhat emotional Uccio (yellow top) and manager Gibo (green beenie) congratulate Vale after witnessing his electrifying win at Donington 2001. (Gold & Goose)

Getting the hang of this four-stroke thing. With team-mate Colin Edwards before their winning ride at the tropically hot Suzuka Eight Hours. (Mark Wernham)

Two weeks later at Assen the pair were brought together to shake hands in front of the cameras, a feat they managed without once looking into each other's eyes. The forced smiles did nothing to soothe their antagonism or hush the apoplectic Italian media, but at least they'd made the effort to convince people that they weren't out to kill each other at this most frightening of racetracks.

Valentino reckons that Assen features the most challenging corner in GP racing, Hoge Heide, where riders must tackle successive waves of camber while negotiating a 160mph right–left flick near the end of the lap. Through the right they ride into a deep dip, suspension fully compressed, before rising out of the dip and heaving the bike left as the suspension fully extends. A moment of deathly silence follows, riders apparently in cruise mode, unable to do anything because the bike is just floating across the tarmac with no grip, so any input would almost certainly cause a big, big crash. But as soon as they descend from that final wave of camber the suspension loads up and they

flick into the 110mph Ramshoek left. It's an impressive sight in qualifying when riders are mostly alone, putting their all into one perfect lap, but in the race, with Vale, Biaggi, Capirossi and Barros locked together in a vicious dogfight, it was frankly terrifying. Someone up there must've known this confrontation might end in disaster, so down came the rain and out came the red flags. Biaggi had been ahead the lap before the race was stopped and was thus declared the winner, Valentino second, Capirossi third.

Robbed of victory and now only 19 points ahead, Valentino and crew headed across the Channel for the British GP where things went from bad to worse. That huge tumble in qualifying left him a dismal 11th on the grid, Max sitting pretty on pole. In the race he bided his time, waiting for the fuel load to lighten before relentlessly working his way toward the front. Race leader Biaggi must've got the shock of his life when his pit board told him who was behind him and within a few laps he too succumbed. At such a crucial stage of the season, when lesser racers might've settled for safe

Biaggi's brave pursuit of Vale's points lead ended at Brno. It was the first of three tumbles that ended his title challenge. (Gold & Goose)

No one's perfect. Valentino was lucky to escape unscathed from this highside-lowside get-off during practice for the Australian GP. (Both Milagro)

points rather than a risky ride to the front, this was a truly inspired ride. And it's right up there in Vale's all-time best races. 'Maybe this was my most exciting victory because I didn't think it was possible to win, so when I crossed the finish line it was the most emotion for me.'

To Japan for Eight Hours tests and then to Germany, where he was back to earth with a bump. If the 2001 NSR was a magnificent motorcycle it soon became obvious that it didn't like the Sachsenring's tortuous twists. Once again he qualified 11th but this time there was no Lazarus-style comeback and he finished the race a crestfallen seventh. Biaggi won at a canter, leading home three other Yamahas, the YZR's sweet-handling chassis lapping up the German curves. Now there were just ten points between them, and all of a sudden the clever money was on Biaggi who had won three of his four 250 titles with storming end-of-season flourishes, while Vale had never been involved in a bruising fight to the finish.

But no time for wailing and gnashing of teeth, just another 12-hour plane ride to Suzuka where he and

Vale assumed a new stature during 2001. Now there was no doubt that he is one of bike racing's all-time greats. (Gold & Goose)

106

Edwards made no mistakes second time around, winning the Eight Hours and returning to the circuit the next morning for something much more important: Valentino's first ride on the all-new RC211V. With Biaggi's YZR500 in the ascendance, here at least was something that might give him some cheer for the future. Not so, Vale declared the test 'a disaster' and returned home to psyche himself up for the Czech GP. In all kinds of ways this would be a crucial encounter. Brno commences the second half of the season after GP racing's summer recess and performances at this epic, high-speed circuit are invariably a good forecast for the remainder of the campaign. During the summer holidays some riders mysteriously fall out of the groove, while others find the speed missing from their earlier outings. So from a purely psychological standpoint it was vital for both riders that they win here. No wonder Valentino considers it the most difficult race of his life.

Ever the master of the artfully fast one-off lap Biaggi claimed pole, just over a tenth up on Valentino, then led the race, his rival quickly slotting in behind. That's how they stayed for some while, Valentino watching and waiting, gathering the information he'd require for an end-of-race attack. 'Biaggi was going so quick and I was thinking, "Ah, maybe it's possible to overtake him here on the last lap", or "Here I'm faster, there I'm slower", and when he crashed I thought "Oh fack, now it's necessary to change my plan".' Biaggi had skated over the edge of the precipice, losing the front and sliding gracefully to earth, then remounting in a panic to salvage a handful of points for tenth. They hardly mattered. The gap was back to 29 points and the scene had been set for the final six races.

'I think Brno is the masterpiece of my career because the mental situation was so difficult before the race, though after Biaggi crashed it wasn't very much exciting.' He followed that with another untroubled win at Estoril where Biaggi covered himself in dust once more, clambering back on board to grimly keep himself on the scoring board. At Valencia Biaggi got his own back, beating Valentino by almost three seconds, but they were only racing for tenth place, the event turned into a tyre lottery by a pre-race downpour.

Leaving Europe behind for the final four 'flyaway' races the gap had swollen to 47 points but Biaggi was not for giving in. He led Valentino at Motegi, only to stumble over the limit once more. Biaggi's pride had been pricked by the run of calamities and turned his wrath not against Valentino but against Yamaha. The YZR chassis, he announced, had a 'structural problem' which didn't allow him to ride as fast as he wanted. He had already complained that Rossi always got lucky, always got the best bikes, conveniently forgetting that he too had been favoured with NSR500 power in '98. But that year he had been in a satellite Honda team and had complained once too often that his equipment didn't match up to Doohan's factory tackle. After that HRC weren't keen to promote him to official team duties, so he switched factories.

Valentino, of course, saw it all differently. There had been no crisis at Yamaha, rather Vale and his crew had been shaken into getting their act together following their disastrous Sachsenring weekend. 'After Germany I told him we wouldn't tolerate the second or third rows anymore,' reveals Burgess. 'I told him he was making great entertainment for the fans but if he wanted to win the championship he'd have to put some pressure on his rival and it's hard to do that from the third row. After that we were only off the front row once all year. We also changed a lot during the next few races: shocks, suspension links, geometry, engine bits, everything, which allowed us to make big improvements in handling.' That's why Biaggi could no longer hack the pace.

'The better parts from HRC helped but it was the team that made the difference because they changed their way of working to suit me,' adds Valentino. 'I use more corner speed than Doohan and you need more accurate settings to ride with my style. So all the suspension settings changed and the bike started to turn better. The Honda 500 had always had a turning problem, it would always run wide, but it was better after Germany.'

Three races to go and the title would be his if he could make the top eight at Phillip Island. Oooh, too tough. Indeed it was, of all the races in which he might have been granted an easy ride, this wasn't it. Phillip Island's fast, swooping curves always encourage elbow-to-elbow racing, but the 2001 Australian GP was an

Dad keeps his promise and loses his pony in celebration. This is the first time he'd had it cut since suffering career-ending head injuries in '82. (Vitali Rosati)

epic amongst Aussie epics, the closest race in over half a century of 500 racing, almost too close. During the early laps Barros and Nori Haga scared the living daylights out of everyone as they duked it out for the lead, Valentino deciding the only safe place was out front after he'd kissed tyres with Barros at 190mph. He didn't stay there long, barging back and forth with Biaggi, Capirossi, Jacque, Nakano and Ukawa. On the final lap it was Max out front by a smidgen but Valentino timed his move to perfection, diving ahead with three corners to go. Less than two seconds separated the first nine riders past the flag, so tactical riding had never been an option and anyway, riding for points isn't his style. Roberts and Criville had won their crowns by doing no more than was absolutely necessary and he wasn't about to emulate them. Burgess, like everyone, was mightily impressed: 'I've always said that if you win races the championships take care of themselves. It's always been that way with the guys I've worked with – Mick, Gardner and Spencer, they all knew how to fight.'

Back home in Iavullia it was almost 6am and the exultant locals were painting the town yellow. Mum wasn't with them though, she'd made the long trip Down Under to celebrate her boy's conquest of motorcycling's highest peak, just 22 years and 240 days after she'd first laid eyes on him.

Valentino isn't the youngest rider to have won the 500 crown, however. Three others have managed it even younger: Freddie Spencer won the 1983 title at 21 years and 258 days, Mike Hailwood secured the 1962 crown aged 22 and 160 days and John Surtees took the 1956 championship at 22 years and 182 days. So what's so special about these guys? What unites them? Riding talent, for a start, towering mountains and raging rivers of the stuff, plus total, unfaltering dedication. (Surtees called his own brand of world-beating determination, 'the inherent Surtees family cussedness'.) And dads that raced bikes: Spencer Senior raced just about anything – dirt bikes, drag bikes, sprint cars, even powerboats – while Hailwood's old man and Surtees' dad raced sidecars before the Second World War. In other words, it all comes down to nature and nurture.

After watching the race in his pyjamas at home, Graziano may well have been pondering this very subject as he popped down the local *barbiere* to have his pony tail cut off in celebration. The cherished pony had been growing ever since he'd emerged shaven-headed from his career-ending coma in September 1982 and here at last was a good enough reason to get rid of the thing. 'It wasn't for a bet, just a display of appreciation and affection,' explains Graziano. 'I told him I'd cut it off if he won all three titles. Every time he's passed to a higher level it's been a pleasurable surprise for me. When he won his first GP in '96 that

The right way to win
the title. Two laps
to go and Vale holds
the advantage over
Biaggi at Phillip
Island...
(Gold & Goose)
...and three minutes
later he was 500
champ, triggering
wild celebrations in
Tavullia where fans
watched the race on
big screens.
(Vitali Rosati)

didn't mean he'd be good at 250s, and 500s are a whole different thing again, so I only realised he's really, really good when he won the 500 championship.'

Moving swiftly on to Sepang the following weekend, Valentino might have been tempted to kick back in the stultifying tropical heat and luxuriate in the glory of it all. Not so, he made the rest look second-rate with a runaway win, having big fun spinning his hot and greasy Michelins well ahead of Capirossi. Incredibly, this was the moment that Valentino reckons he finally mastered the 500: 'In Malaysia I finally arrive to go very fast with the 500.' And this 38th win took him into the all-time top nine GP winners' list.

Just one race to go before the end of the 500 era and surely there was only one man who should win it. But conditions could scarcely have been trickier at Rio, the rain coming and going, Valentino crossing the finish line second, a fraction down on Checa, but still winning. How so? The race had been interrupted by a rain shower and run in two parts, the result decided on aggregate. Valentino crossed the finish line a metre behind the Spaniard but had a two tenths advantage in hand from the first leg. To add indignity to defeat, he'd done it running the wrong tyres – squirming intermediates against his rival's noticeably grippier cut slicks. Chubby Checa's look of abject misery upon the podium spoke for everyone: 'Just what do we have to do to beat this guy?'.

Of course, there was one man he'd never beaten – Doohan. So could he beat the biggest, baddest of the Old Dogs? 'I've seen some of Mick's data readouts and, fack, he was very fast. It was him that made the difference, not the bike. If I was to race Mick, I think I could fight with him, but I don't know who would win. Nobody knows!' Burgess also sits on the fence on this one: 'I wouldn't like to say Valentino's got more talent than Mick, I've seen Mick do some pretty special things on a motorcycle.'

And what if Valentino rode a Yamaha, could he still beat Max? 'Biaggi gave 120 per cent to beat me in 2001, so the fight was facking hard. In the past he never rode the 500 like that. For me, I think I could beat him with Yamaha because we're not talking about Biaggi winning six races and me seven, or me scoring just ten points more than him. Of course, I think my bike is very good, but I also think that I was the fastest rider of 2001, usually. I won 11 races, Biaggi won three and he only won Assen because the race was stopped early. And when he won at Le Mans and Sachsenring his team-mate Checa was second, so for sure those tracks were not so bad for the Yamaha; at Sachsenring there were five Yamahas in the first six!'

Not that the relative differences between the YZR and NSR mattered any more, because 500s were about to be consigned to history, although Valentino wasn't happy about that because he didn't reckon the RCV was going to be as fun to ride. In fact he kept suggesting he might stick with the NSR in 2002, although he was only kidding himself. Honda had been a prime mover in the shift to four-strokes, so there was no way they were going to let their number one rider continue racing a 'stinkwheel'.

RCV testing began alongside new team-mate Ukawa at Jerez in November, a whole army of HRC engineers descending on the Andalucian track, praying that the work they'd done since July would be to their champion's liking. It wasn't. 'The bike still wasn't very good but we made a good test at Jerez. I'm good at understanding what I want from the bike and HRC are very good at giving me what I want. After Jerez everything changed: the cowling, the seat, the engine character, all the electronic parts, it was a new bike by

the start of the 2002 season.'

In other words, maybe the RCV wouldn't have become the weapon it did without Valentino's unique input. Your average rider works on machine set-up one adjustment at a time, so if the bike turns better, keeps its line better or is more stable, he'll know what caused that improvement, so his crew can make further adjustments in that direction and perhaps make the bike even better. If his crew were to change several things at once – say one click on the front rebound damping, two clicks on the rear compression and a different construction front tyre – the rider couldn't be sure which of these changes affected performance, so his crew can't go on from there. Valentino is different. 'He has some kind of amazing link system which allows him to think "I like this" and "I don't like this",' explains Fiorani. 'So he can test many different things at the same time without getting confused.' This is just another part of his talent for riding a motorcycle ridiculously fast – it's not just riding ability, it's his pit-lane brain that helps him improve the bike, so he can employ even more of his talent on the track.

During the Jerez tests Valentino did at least break his own 500 record, although recently crowned 250 champ Daijiro Kato was also there, getting into the swing of things with his NSR500s, and he went even faster. This was the first hint that the two-strokes might not roll over and die the moment the four-strokes hit the track. Ever since Checa had ridden Yamaha's YZR-M1 four-stroke to a blindingly fast simulated race time during private tests at Brno in August, the 500s had looked dead and gone. But here was evidence to suggest that reports of their demise had been greatly exaggerated. Around tighter and slower tracks the four-strokes seemed unable to fully exploit their 200-plus horsepower engines while the two-strokes could capitalise on their lighter weight.

Four wheels were next, and he put on an impressive display in Michelin's Race of Champions rally event on Gran Canaria where he made it to the quarter finals, only losing out to World Rally star Alistair McRae. People were already suggesting he'd quit bikes in a year or two to go full-time rallying. 'If I win with the four-stroke maybe it will be necessary to change sport,

A taste of the future'? Vale loves driving cars almost as much as riding bikes. And he impressed the pros in Michelin's Gran Canaria rally event at the end of 2001. (Michelin)

'For sure there is more good than bad to being famous.' Vale makes a new friend during the Michelin Race of Champions rally event, 2001. (Michelin)

and after bikes rallying is my passion, but to say I'll do the World Rally after bikes is unreal, because, fack, you have people who've been racing rallies for 25 years, while I'd be starting from zero, so I don't know if I can be fast enough.'

Meanwhile, HRC returned to their Asaka HQ to further refine the RCV, agreeing to meet Valentino at Sepang in late January. But the test never happened. In early January the two parties fell out over a new two-year contract, reputed to be worth £10 million. 'In December we understand we are still a little too far away, so we need time to change something in the contract about our point of view and something about Honda's point of view. But the biggest problem is that all the Italian journalists write too much, is not true that the argument was about Honda wanting me to use number one, not 46. We had already finished that discussion before the end of 2001 season. No, we have other problem but is better we don't say; is secret.'

The disagreement forced Vale to cancel his holidays and stay in London, hunkering down with Gibo, firing off faxes and emails and working on his new look: shaggy-dog hair, bewhiskered face and a military green forage cap, like a youthful Fidel Castro. Very cool. 'I begin to look like a wolf and in March my mother say I can't come in her house!' He also acquired a deep tan from somewhere, certainly not from London's winter sun. 'Is not real sun, is lamp! My girls like it!' And we thought Biaggi was the vain one…

The contract bickering was resolved in time for the next tests at Sepang in early February, where he demolished the 500 race record he'd established in October, giving HRC a timely reminder of his worth. News of the RCV's devastating speed raised blood pressure in race shops around Japan and Italy, especially in Iwata where Yamaha were toiling away on their M1. Biaggi and Checa had tested the M1 at Sepang during December and neither had gone as quick. But lap times exacted from private tests are often misleading because track

conditions vary from day to day and because the numbers can be pure propaganda. So no one was quite sure whether HRC were giving it some spin, until the first group teams' test at Catalunya in early March when Valentino came out well on top, Ukawa and Capirossi the only ones even close. And Capirossi was riding his 2001-spec NSRs like a maniac: little body hunched forward, grimly hanging on as the bike took on a life of its own, all crossed up and pointing any which way but straight.

The same deal during final pre-season tests at Suzuka; Valentino well ahead and Capirossi already proclaiming him World Champion. 'Loris say that with the RCV I can win the title riding with one hand, maybe I will try that later,' he joked. Suzuka race weekend was no walkover, however. He crashed twice in practice, destroying one of his RCVs on the Saturday. This was surely a wake-up call for someone straying dangerously close to the foggy realm of over-confidence, like someone was still up there, looking out for

him. The crashes were big ones. On Friday he lost the front at 120mph, bloodying his hands as he scrubbed off speed before ricocheting off the trackside barriers, then the next morning he took such a wide line into Degner Two that he ran off the track on the outside as he peeled in. This was playing way too fast and loose with his cornering lines.

Suitably chastened, he only just scraped into pole position, his rivals much closer than pre-season lap times had predicted. And on Sunday he rode a careful, well-thought-out race in sodden conditions, learning the best rain lines from local Akira Ryo before moving ahead to win the first race of the new four-stroke era. The victory was also Honda's first four-stroke GP success since their original racing era ended in 1967, so not only was the shift of eras helping to build his legend, it was also making Honda love him even more. Newly appointed HRC president Suguru Kanazawa emphasised the significance of the success: 'Winning GPs with four-stroke machinery has always been our

Different bike, same result. Valentino and RCV head Ryo, Itoh and Checa at rain-lashed Suzuka. (Gold & Goose)

The race queen gets it – celebrating on the Suzuka podium with runner-up Ryo. (Gold & Goose)

goal, so today's victory is very meaningful to me and everyone else at Honda.' Kanazawa had been working towards this day ever since he'd left university in the late Seventies and designed the exotic, oval-pistoned NR500 four-stroke, which was humiliated by the then-dominant Yamaha and Suzuki two-strokes.

Suzuka, however, proved to be a useless season forecast. First, the RCV was in fact much further ahead of its rivals than it had appeared in Japan, and second, Valentino wasn't going to win every one of the year's 16 races. At Welkom, he and Ukawa finished almost half a minute ahead of the pack, Capirossi the only man anywhere near their pace and flirting with disaster at every corner. But it was an unusually bad day for Vale. He chose a too-soft rear slick that couldn't match Ukawa's harder compound during the closing stages, then made two cock-ups on the final lap which allowed the Japanese through to win.

The result was reminiscent of Doohan's three 'tow truck' defeats in 1996 and '97 when the great Aussie was beaten by Repsol Honda team-mates Alex Criville and Tady Okada who doggedly stuck to his tailpipes then skidded past on the final lap. Doohan reserved his deepest scorn for these tactics and communicated his feelings with a look of thunder while standing on the podium. Valentino just kept on grinning. As Schwantz and others have observed, he can handle getting beat once in a while. In fact, he had looked much more traumatised earlier in the week at Welkom during a heart-breaking visit to a local kids-with-HIV centre. Valentino is a genius motorcycle rider, but human in every way – vulnerable and beatable – which is why everyone loves the guy.

Old 250 rival Ukawa sticks to Valentino's tailpipes as the RCV duo lay waste to Capirossi & Co at Welkom. Ukawa was the surprise winner. (Gold & Goose)

On a hot lap
during qualifying,
Mugello 2001.
(Gold & Goose)

how Rossi rides

Grand prix bikes are the baddest-assed motorcycles on Earth because they've got more brakes, more grip, more rigid chassis and, most crucially, more horse-power than anything else. Valentino has to constantly juggle body weight and throttle input to get his RCV on to the fattest part of the tyre, so he can rip as much horsepower as possible through that contact patch, all the while keeping the rear tyre spinning, not too little, not just too much. Too little wheelspin means he's not laying down enough power and not helping the bike to turn, too much wheelspin and he's losing forward drive or he's about to have a highside.

Like only the greatest racers, Valentino keeps the thing dancing on that precipice, using everything just as hard as he can, so if he braked any later, cornered any faster, accelerated any harder, he'd go over the edge. Like any pro-racer, he makes a living out of being given an inch and trying to make it a mile, but his own personal precipice is many miles on from our own, and even out there his control is so much more deft, even when the bike's skipping and sliding beneath him, like it does into every corner, through every corner and out of every corner.

Someone like Valentino inhabits a world that's difficult to compare with our own because his experience of bike riding is so alien to ours, but maybe you can have a go at imagining for a moment that you're a GP rider. Let's say that you're in the closing stages of the British GP and you're rocketing into the first turn at 155mph, there's someone to the left of you and someone to the right, the guy on the right has just barged past and nicked your line, brakes squealing, suspension juddering,

Honda's RCV is possibly the most powerful race bike ever and yet Vale had little problem getting to grips with the beast. (Gold & Goose)

tyres chattering as he ricochets off your bike and nearly rips your right hand off the 'bars.

Your front tyre is tucking, pushing and sliding as you tip into the turn, so you're thrusting your right knee deep into the tarmac to keep some weight off the over-worn tyre, at the same time as you're thinking about getting on the throttle. You crack the throttle a fraction, just to get the revs building and take some more weight off the front, then you open it some more, until you can feel the rear tyre loading up, then you open it some more until you feel the revs rise and the tyre getting all greasy and braking loose, so you ease off and push like a bastard on the outside footpeg until the rubber regains some traction, which you immediately eat up by getting back on the throttle, which pushes the bike wide until you're on the rumble strip, so you ease off again as the tyre jumps, spins and kicks back across the kerb. Now you're pushing back in the seat to get more weight on that rear tyre and weighting the 'pegs to complete the cornering arc to the right, which takes you back on to the tarmac where the rear tyre grips and kicks the front wheel into the air, so you pull your weight over the front of the bike,

easing the throttle for a millisecond, trying to get the front back on the tarmac as you head down towards Craner Curves, your hands, feet, backside and brain in some kind of a St Vitus dance of a balancing act as you lean hard right at 130mph, all of three feet behind the guy who's just overtaken you.

That's one breathless snapshot of maybe five seconds in a GP that lasts 45 minutes. In other words, a GP is just like that, except repeated about 550 times, and I've mentioned only the most basic inputs that a rider uses through each and every corner. The really scary thing is that a rider like Valentino has made the most intricate of adjustments to all of those inputs every time he's switched bikes, from 125s to 250s, from 250s to 500s and from 500s to 1,000cc four-strokes. Somehow he has been able to reach into his subconscious, then override and reconfigure each facet of his riding technique, and all this while all hell is breaking loose on the racetrack.

His achievement is unique in bike racing history. In more than 50 years of GPs only one other rider has secured the triple crown of 125, 250 and 500 titles and that was Briton Phil Read, who took ten years to

Rossano Brazzi gives Vale his first lesson in 250 riding at Jerez, late '97. (Milagro)

Throttle control is everything on a 190hp motorcycle: Vale, Capirossi and Barros burn some rubber at Sachsenring 2001. (Gold & Goose)

ろっしぃうす
がんばって！

HRC
How is my drive? Call 0039-0652-3891

'How is my drive?' Pretty good, actually. (Gold & Goose)

The Aprilia was always more difficult to get off the line than the Hondas and Yamahas of Capirossi (1), Nakano (56) and Ukawa (4). Capirossi won this Assen race from Valentino. (Gold & Goose)

conquer the different classes, almost twice as long as the youngster. Valentino's ability to adapt so quickly marks him out as a superman among supermen, and one of the most versatile riders ever. So what is this talent with which he is blessed?

Every rider has his own style, his own way of controlling a motorcycle via throttle control, body weight and maximising traction. But different types of motorcycle require very different techniques to extract maximum performance from their engines and chassis. Valentino has the ability to swap seamlessly from one bike to another because he's been riding all kinds of bikes for 20 years, because he inherited the right genes from his GP-winning dad and because he's a bit of a genius. He's not quite unique, of course, men like King Kenny Roberts ruled American dirt track before conquering 500 GPs, and Sixties' legend Mike Hailwood could win three different GP classes in a day, though the specifics of different racing categories were less back then. But most riders are much less able to achieve the same level of competitiveness with different types of machine – witness the many 250 and Superbike stars who have failed to reinvent themselves as 500 heroes. These riders develop their skills and technique as they master a particular type of machine, but when they change classes, their style won't change with them.

Riding technique is a largely subconscious function, so it's hard to know exactly what you're doing a lot of the time, because there's so much going on when you're teetering on the limit, duelling with a rival. To be able to adapt the way you brake, turn, accelerate, shift your body weight and so on therefore demands a very special mind. Valentino, being a modest guy, shrugs it all off. 'Racing 125s was like a game, 250s were serious, but 500s are very serious!' he said halfway through his first 500 season. 'They're dangerous: you open the throttle and you've got almost 200 horse-power, so you have to be careful…'

Niall Mackenzie, who won the British 250 title, then went on to score several 500 GP podiums before returning to dominate the national Superbike scene, believes Valentino's secret is threefold: his lack of an 'I know best' ego which allows him to look, listen and learn, his ability to rear-wheel steer and his refusal to hang around in any one class too long.

'The longer you stay on one kind of bike, the harder it is to change,' says Mackenzie. 'Rossi wasn't on 250s too long and even when he was he looked like he was already thinking about how to ride 500s. He seems prepared to change how he rides, while most other riders decide their way is the only way.

'When I was riding 500s I'd be competitive if the bike or my style suited the track but that doesn't work every week, you have to be able to adapt and that's where the Americans and Australians scored when I was riding, and where Rossi scores now. They ride the rear wheel because you can give the rear so much more abuse and get away with it. If you rely on the front there's such a fine line between the tyres gripping, to allow you to keep up your corner speed, and crashing. On a 125 you can push the front all day long, maybe a little less on a 250, but 500s push the front so much harder, because you've got more weight and a huge rear-tyre contact patch.'

Californian Wayne Rainey, who won three 500 titles while Mackenzie struggled to get the best out of 500s,

Exploring the limit at Mugello, midway through his first GP season. (Gold & Goose)

was the master of slide. 'As a kid, being sideways was as normal as riding in a straight line,' says Rainey, who grew up doing US dirt track. 'When I started roadracing in the early Eighties, I didn't know if sliding was right or wrong but it was what I felt comfortable with. If the tyre wasn't spinning and the bike turning, I didn't feel right. I liked it spinning because it gives you a safety buffer, you kinda know where you can go with it.

'In fact, sliding is the easy part, the difficult part is front-tyre feel. The key to my riding style was getting through that area really quick, getting the front tyre out of the way so I could get on the throttle. When you brake and flick, it's all front tyre, which is kinda risky. The advantage rear-wheel steering gave me was huge. And it's just the same now – watch Rossi, he's getting a bit sideways now. It's great when you've a lot of grip because you can use more throttle than the other guys, and then when the grip starts to fade, you know where the traction is.

'To me the throttle was everything. But when you're doing this you're talking very small changes in throttle opening because you're at the limit of everything – throttle position, chassis flex, tyre flex, you're feeling all that stuff. Spinning the rear relieves pressure on the tyre, relieves pressure on the suspension and that widens the safety area. But you're only spinning to keep the bike turning, just to keep it on track. Most of the time you don't want the tyre to spin much at all, you want it to drive maximum, you're always focused on drive.'

Valentino's mentor, Mick Doohan, played his part in helping the youngster adapt to big bikes but the former 500 champ insists that Valentino did most of the work himself. 'He has studied everyone, from Freddie Spencer to the guys he races against now,' says Doohan. 'He looks at them all on TV and works out the best way to ride. He's watched so many races on video that he probably knows them better than the statistics guys. He watches, he thinks and he listens to others. I told him a few things early on – not to keep the bike on its side so much, just get it into the turn, get it up and get it out – but it didn't take him long to catch on.'

Whatever his god-given talent, Valentino needed to change his riding style when he came to 500s. He'd grown up through 125s and 250s, where corner speed is king, and while corner speed is also crucial in big-bike racing, it's not the way to ride from start to finish. A 200hp motorcycle burns up its tyres during a race, so the sidegrip that is there in the early laps isn't there later on. Watch Valentino accelerate out of a turn and he does exactly what Doohan advised him to do – he lifts the bike, almost violently, as he brings on the throttle, which gives him a larger tyre-to-tarmac contact patch that can handle bigger throttle openings.

Adjusting to that corner-exit style requires the rider to use less corner speed, so he's got to adapt by slowing down, obviously a very difficult thing for any racer to do since this is the opposite of their remit. To succeed on a 500 you must breach that mental barrier

and slow your corner entry so you can focus on corner exit, raise the bike on to the fatter section of its rear tyre and then open that throttle, little by little. That's how Valentino transformed himself from 250 winner to big-bike king, by using less corner speed, much more intricate throttle control and a willingness to adapt his technique throughout the race, according to fuel load and tyre wear.

'It's really difficult because your head's telling you that the rear-end style seems slow,' continues Mackenzie. 'In a race you're in an intense, urgent situation, so you're just thinking "Fast, fast, keep going fast!", your brain is telling you to rush into corners, so you're pushing the front for more corner speed. You've got to force yourself to slow down but you're thinking "Using the rear and not pushing the front is slow, if I do that I'm going to lose time and places".

'Somehow you've got to have some kind of mechanism within yourself to override what feels fast and what is fast, that's the clever bit, that's the tricky bit. Guys like Rainey and Doohan could ride the rear too, because it came naturally from riding the dirt. If you can force yourself to keep riding the rear, eventually you'll go faster, although the longer you've been doing high corner speed, the harder it is to stop.'

Which brings us to Max Biaggi. Rossi's arch-rival challenged for the 2001 500 title after three wins at tracks well suited to his high corner speed style but his brave effort collapsed after three copycat front-end crashes. The theory goes that Biaggi stayed in 250s too long, lording it over his rivals with the number-one plate, so that by the time he got to 500s he couldn't change (although he'd argue that he challenged Doohan for the title in his first 500 season, when he was riding Hondas, suggesting it's his Yamaha that was at fault).

'Biaggi is a very hard 250 rider and he's also very good on 500s,' says Valentino. 'But you never see him slide the rear because he uses the front so much. When I started 500s I also used the front very much and I crashed many times.'

Mackenzie likens Rossi's adaptability to that of Doohan, who won five 500 titles after a near-crippling accident which left him more disabled than he ever lets on. 'Rossi's ability to think and adapt compares to the way Mick coped with his right foot not moving. He forced himself to adapt, to ride the bike with a really weak right leg and with no movement in his right ankle. Most other riders would say: "I just can't do this, it's not physically possible". It's hard enough to ride a 500 when you're 100 per cent, so it's easy to say "I can't ride it properly now", but Doohan forced his way around that.'

Valentino admits to using Doohan's riding style as a reference point, but he hasn't simply copied every aspect of the grand master's technique. 'Mick used to slide and go, like a real 500 rider, and his settings didn't have to be so exact because of that,' he explains. 'But I came from 250s so I had to change my style to go into

Chasing Ueda's Honda 125 in '97 and using maximum mid-corner speed to take him on to the next straight as fast as possible.
(Gold & Goose)

'It feels like this.' Getting the point across to Joe Skid, Vale's Ohlins suspensions technician during his 250 days. (Henk Keulemans)

corners a little slower, and though I learned to understand slide control and started to slide like Mick, I'm still faster in the middle of the corner, not because I'm a better rider, just because I have a different technique.'

Nevertheless, Doohan has nothing but praise for Rossi's technique: 'I think Valentino is the only guy who rides right at the moment. The rest of them ride like they're on 250s, so when the tyres go off they've got no answer, their only answer is to roll off the throttle. In qualifying, everyone goes quick because they've got fresh tyres and low fuel loads, but come halfway through the race, when the front tyre starts to push and the rear starts to spin, they've got to slow down but Valentino adjusts his riding style to accommodate the change in grip, moving his body weight differently and using the throttle differently. That's where he's got it, that's why he's consistently quick from lap one to lap 30.'

Mackenzie is amazed that Valentino mastered sideways corner exits so quickly. 'He seems to slide the rear so easily, though he's got a very ordinary riding style, like some guy at a track day, but he's obviously using his weight, balance and throttle control. It's pretty obvious what he was doing on the 500 during 2001. He'd be with them for the first half of the race, watching, waiting and probably pretty much at his limit. But during the second half, when everyone else's fronts were shot, so they couldn't push hard anymore, then he'd start riding the rear.'

Valentino's rear-wheel-steering ability is the result of a very special natural talent that has been honed since the day he first rode a minibike aged two and a half. Again, he shrugs it off: 'I think my throttle control is just

Moving into 250s required slowing his mid-corner speed and focusing more on corner exits.
(Gold & Goose)

natural. I started very young and rode many bikes but I don't know why I have this style of control. When me and Loris Capirossi were racing 250s for Aprilia, he used the throttle like a switch, on or off, I use more gentle control, but he was usually just as fast.' Maybe on 250s, but Valentino's ultra-delicate throttle control makes all the difference when you're dealing with double the horsepower. When he came to 500 GPs in 2000 it took just a couple of races before his data-logging traces told Honda that his throttle control was far superior to that of their more experienced riders like Capirossi, Alex Criville and Tady Okada.

But Valentino's corner-exit secret isn't just throttle control. It's also the intricate feel he possesses, so he knows what the rear tyre is going to do, almost before it does it.

'To slide like they do, GP riders need a huge amount of feel and feedback,' explains Michelin's bike racing boss Nicolas Goubert. 'They need to sense exactly what the tyre is doing, and from experience, know what it's going to do next. Tyre compound and, to a lesser extent, construction are the crucial factors in offering excellent feedback.

'The more grip a rider has at his disposal, the more feel and feedback he needs. What most riders want is a period of warning as they approach the limit. It's no good having massive amounts of grip if the limit is reached without any warning, because the rider won't have the confidence to approach that limit. Most riders will go faster with slightly less grip and more feedback. Only the very best riders can go fastest with a huge amount of grip and minimal feedback, because their skill allows them to cope with less of a transition phase.'

Superbike star Chris Walker's fated attempt to conquer the 500 class in 2001 was spent in awe of men like Valentino. 'When I followed good 500 guys into corners, I could sometimes run up on them a little, even the best riders out there. But by the time I came out of the turn, they were halfway down the next straight! The good 500 guys seem to turn the corner more, then pick up the bike and get on the gas really hard. With Superbikes you spend a lot more time on your side, so on the 500 I'd find I was always leant over further than anyone else. With a four-stroke you can actually get on the power while the bike is on its side. A Superbike weighs more, so there's more weight on the tyres when it's leaned over, so there's obviously more grip, and the power is less aggressive, much smoother, so you can drive out of the corner. The 500 is very different – they're so aggressive when the power comes on tap, that you go from good grip to zero grip virtually instantly.'

That's the real difference between a hard man and a hero, between a good GP rider and a legend: super-intricate throttle control that allows the rider to unleash maximum horsepower impossibly early out of every corner. Valentino has dedicated most of his life to honing that skill and now reaps the rewards.

'It feels like that'. Deep in hi-tech discussions with Jeremy Burgess and his 500 crew. (Gold & Goose)

Getting down with Honda's user-friendly SP-1 Superbike at the 2001 Suzuka Eight Hour. (Mark Wernham)

VALENTINO PEACE & LOVE

DIESEL

RADIO DEE JAY

The bodywork of
a race bike is a
crucial
aerodynamic aid
to increased
performance. For
Valentino, it's also
an empty canvas.
(Gold & Goose)

Rossi's weapons

Rossi's new world
Honda RCV 2002

Honda made its name winning GPs with exotic four-stroke race bikes, and for the first time in 35 years the world's biggest bike manufacturer is back doing that with its RCV V5. Honda has always been a four-stroke brand, indeed company founder Soichiro Honda hated smelly, smoky two-strokes so much that his R&D engineers used to explain away two-stroke blueprints as lawnmower engines.

Honda's speciality always was exotica; during the Sixties the company's engineers produced a twin-cylinder 50cc GP bike, a five-cylinder 125 and a 250 six, all revving beyond 20,000rpm; no wonder Honda's first nine years of GP racing yielded 16 riders' world championships, 18 constructors' crowns and 138 victories. But during the Seventies, two-stroke technology advanced to the extent that not even Honda could compete with its outrageous 32-valve, oval-pistoned NR500 four-stroke, so the company went with the two-stroke flow, winning a further 25 riders' titles and 35 constructors' crowns between 1983 and 2001.

Now Honda is back to doing what it does best thanks to a transformation of Grand Prix regulations designed to put four-strokes out front and consign two-strokes to the history books. This seismic shift was somewhat inevitable, given the environmental concerns that have marginalised the two-stroke engine as a practicable power source for streetbikes. The new four-stroke MotoGP series thus brings the world's premier race series in line with the global street market,

Honda RCV 2002	
Engine specifications	
Type	liquid-cooled 20-valve, 75.5° V5 four-stroke
Displacement	990cc
Fuel system	PGM fuel injection
Claimed output	around 220hp
Gearbox	six-speed, cassette type
Chassis specifications	
Frame type	dual beam aluminium
Tyres	Michelin
Wheels	17in front, 16.5in rear
Front brake	four-pot Brembo, twin carbon discs (dry), twin cast-iron discs (wet)
Rear-brake	two-pot Brembo, single disc
Front suspension	upside down Showa, multi-adjustable
Rear suspension	unit Pro-link with Showa shock, multi-adjustable
Wheelbase	1,440mm
Length	2,050mm
Race weight	over 145kg

Motorcycle as art:
HRC know how to
build a GP bike.
Note massive
swingarm.
(Gold & Goose)

delivering more direct feedback to streetbike development and allowing factories to more fully exploit their
racing success in the marketplace.

The new rules admit 990cc four-strokes to GP
racing, giving them engines twice as big as the existing
500s. But Valentino wasn't an immediate convert to the
four-stroke cause. During his two seasons with his
NSR500 two-stroke he developed a deep love for the
bike's razor-edged power delivery and initially found
the easier-going RCV uninspiring to ride. Then he
checked the lap times …

Short, stubby and very businesslike, the RCV is
probably the most powerful Grand Prix bike ever built.
The five-cylinder vee makes a booming off-kilter racket
and produces around 220hp, maybe 20 or 30 more than
the NSR that Valentino raced to the 2001 500
Championship, so it didn't take long for him to surpass
his NSR lap times.

'The RCV is incredible,' he says. 'The first time I
tested it at Suzuka after the Eight Hour in July 2001 it
was a bit of a disaster, the bike was too small, many
things weren't right for me. Valentino's main concerns

were to make the cramped riding position more accommodating and to tame the too-direct power delivery. 'When I first rode the RCV, it would spin the rear tyre leaving the pits!' he adds.

Now Valentino's only gripe is the bike's rather modest Manga cartoon-inspired bodywork, he keeps complaining about its meagre fairing, and so would you at 200mph. The RCV does indeed look seriously unaerodynamic but is it? In some ways, yes, in some ways, no. The kind of swoopy bodywork required to slice through the air in a straight line actually compromises performance in other areas, causing instability during braking and cornering, especially in high-speed turns. The tight, angular fairing therefore improves lap times and it doesn't matter if the RCV's straight-line speed is compromised because Honda have never had a problem squeezing more horsepower out of their engines than anyone else.

The RCV is a distillation of everything that Honda has learned from racing in almost half a century of competition, and yet the bike's V5 configuration was anything but an obvious choice for the new four-stroke championship. But Honda has always believed that taking the more difficult road can earn them greater knowledge, although this insistence on being different has sometimes cost Honda dear. Back in the late Seventies they tried to take on the all-dominant two-stroke 500s with the NR and never scored a single world championship point despite blowing billions of yen. Then, in the mid-Eighties their first NSR500 ran its fuel tank under the engine, with the aim of lowering the centre of gravity, but the bike was a disaster.

'We aim to prove that Honda technology is better than the easy way, like inline four,' says Honda Racing Corporation director Yasuo Ikenoya. 'People ask us why we chose the difficult way but the answer is simple: racing is meant to be a challenge, and racing is in Honda's DNA. Of course, we considered other configurations. A V4 would be good – short and narrow – but a V4 is not interesting to us!'

Burgess reckons Honda are ahead because they didn't compromise when they designed the RCV. 'I really think that it's better to start with a clean sheet of paper, then you don't have to make any compromises,' he says.

'Honda started from nowhere when they began work, then they did enough research to see what's the best tool to work within the regulations. Yamaha and Suzuki both shoehorned their four-stroke motors into modified 500 chassis, and that's a compromise.'

The straight-talking Aussie, who's never been afraid to tell his Japanese bosses what he thinks when they do get things wrong, also believes that HRC were correct in choosing a five-cylinder engine. MotoGP regs have a sliding scale of minimum weight limits: the more cylinders, the higher the minimum weight, but fours and fives share the same 145kg limit. 'If you can run the same weight as a four, you might as well have a five,' he adds, 'So the five was definitely the right way to go.'

Honda also considered building a V6 but the new four-stroke regs place a further 10kg weight handicap on bikes using six or more cylinders. Honda have heavily emphasised the concept of total balance with the RCV. 'Total balance' is racing's current buzz phrase and isn't difficult to grasp. Outright horsepower isn't the way to win races nowadays, especially in four-stroke GPs, because all the bikes have more than enough horsepower. What counts is how that power is made to work with the rest of the bike – the chassis and, most crucially, the tyres.

'The RCV combines all our racing experience to produce optimum power with good machine control,' Ikenoya goes on. 'There are three elements to our total balance concept: concentration of mass, minimal frontal area and optimum traction. All the riders that have ridden the bike have been impressed by its power and compactness.'

Compactness is a driving force with the RCV, hence the narrowish vee angle of 75.5°. The more compact you make the motor, the more room you have to put the engine where you want it, focusing the centre of mass.

HRC have further followed that concept by mounting the fuel tank as low as possible. That's obviously what Honda were trying to do when they built the 'upside-down' NSR500 in 1984, but they went too far that time. Instead of gaining from a low c of g, they suffered for it, because their engineers didn't realise that pitch is crucial for adjusting traction between the front and rear tyres as the rider goes in and out of a corner.

The RCV's fuel tank isn't that low; it's positioned very centrally, partly under the front of the seat, a clever feature that helps to banish the excessive pitch suffered by machines with conventional tanks, especially on full fuel loads early in the race.

'In the past all our riders have complained about riding with full fuel tanks,' adds Ikenoya. 'You could see that Rossi was always very fast at the end of races when his NSR500's fuel load was less, we wanted him to be fast from the early laps and the RCV's fuel tank design helps in this way.'

It would be gross understatement to suggest that the RCV is easy to ride, but the bike is certainly less demanding than the old NSR, which is why the new breed of four-strokes are generically quicker around a racetrack than 500s.

'The four-stroke is easier because when you're mid-corner on a 500 you have zero power,' says Valentino's engineer Jerry Burgess. 'When you open the throttle from the lowest rpm point, say 6,000, the 500's not making any more power than a streetbike, but then it suddenly builds to 190hp. With the four-stroke you touch the throttle mid-corner and you've still got tons of torque, so from that point you can open the throttle fairly quickly, whereas with two-strokes you have to be

really careful how you open the throttle.' In fact, it's not quite as simple as that. Early in the RCV's development phase Valentino found that the RCV had too much low-rpm torque, so much so that it'd kick the bike sideways the moment he touched the throttle at maximum lean, so he got HRC to tinker with the torque curve.

Towards the upper reaches of its rev range the RCV is all about brute horsepower – in fact there's never been a more powerful GP bike. 'The engine is just bloody fast,' adds JB. 'There's so much power that you can just drive past a 500, even on a short straight.'

And there are other advantages. Four-strokes have much more engine braking than two-strokes, which gives better traction and improved feel on a closed throttle. We'll leave a rival engineer, Garry McCoy's former crew chief, Hamish Jamieson, to explain this one.

'I think there's a few reasons why four-strokes are easier,' says Jamieson. 'They're heavier for a start, which makes them easier, because they're less flighty. They've more weight and inertia, so they're less of a handful to control, while 500s are barely touching the ground half the time, so they've got no grip.

'In the Red Bull Yamaha team we had a good example in Nori Haga coming to 500s from Superbikes

If Valentino was sad to see the back of the NSR, it didn't take him too long to fall in love with the RCV.
(James Wright)

RCV's low-slung fuel tank has a low c of y because Vale found the fully gassed-up NSR a handful in the early stages of races.
(Gold & Goose)

in 2001. He found the 500 difficult to turn in because there's no engine braking. A 500 doesn't slow down with stability from the rear the way a four-stroke does. Getting a 500 stopped and turned is difficult because the bike just wants to go straight on, and if you get the front to stop, the rear wants to come around. With a 500, there's this transition period when the rider has finished braking but he's not opened the throttle, so the bike's loose, it's not taut like a four-stroke, it's just running free, a bit out of control. That's why guys like Haga and Chris Walker struggled on 500s.'

But four-strokes aren't all good. According to minimum weight regulations the V5 must weigh 15kg more than a 500, and that's a huge difference in racetrack terms. 'And the weight is also in different places compared to the 500,' adds Burgess. 'So the RCV doesn't turn as fast as the 500 and Valentino can't flick it left and right so quick, plus it's fuel injected, so it's a whole new game.'

Of course, too much engine braking can be a bad thing, but HRC have got that well and truly sussed with their four-stroke racers. They developed the so-called back-torque limiter for the high-revving NR500, to minimise rear-wheel hop into corners, and have perfected the design in recent years.

Burgess again: 'The RCV's slipper clutch is just another setting part for us, we can dial it out for some tracks, so we've no engine braking, and dial it in for others.'

The RCV's five-cylinder configuration helps here too. Some of Honda's four-stroke GP rivals have struggled with excessive engine braking unsettling their machines as they hurtle into corners, seriously affecting lap times. 'The five is definitely a help on engine braking,' adds Burgess. 'Way back I had an old Honda CB750 four road bike and I could kick start it with my hand, you couldn't do that with a Norton twin. It follows that you're going to have less compression at any one time if you've got five strokes per two engine revolutions rather than four, and that's got to help any engine-braking problems.'

If the RCV gives Valentino an easier ride on the racetrack, it also gives Burgess and his crew an easier time in the pits. No longer do they have to fully strip and rebuild engines, as they did with the NSR because RCV engines are prepared away from the racetrack. Also, the bike's fuel injection system means no more fiddling around with carburettor jets, and the four-stroke's wider rpm range means less mucking about with gearbox ratios. Easy life!

Maximum respect
Honda NSR500
2000/2001

Valentino's Nastro Azzurro Honda NSR500 was the last and greatest of the two-stroke 500s that ruled Grand Prix racing for quarter of a century, from 1975 to 2001. The machine was the apogee of the high-performance two-stroke racer, a 190hp, 130kg surface-to-surface missile that could be safely and successfully guided only by the sharpest, bravest riders.

Valentino has more respect for the NSR than any other motorcycle he's ridden. 'I think it's necessary to have big balls to ride the 500,' he says. 'The four-stroke RCV may be faster but for sure it doesn't give same sensation. Yes, the satisfaction of riding the 500 was a very, very big motivation for me, because when you're riding the most difficult bike in the world, it's necessary to have a perfect set-up if you're to be able to ride fast, and you've also got to ride perfect all the time.'

By the time Valentino graduated to 500s in 2000, the NSR500 had been developed into the most successful 500 GP bike ever. Mick Doohan alone won 54 GPs on it between 1990 and '98, and Valentino's 13 500 wins took the NSR to 132 GP victories. During his ten GP seasons, Mighty Mick helped make the NSR almost unbeatable, but Valentino made the best bike in the world even better in his two years with the machine. The guy has divine riding talent and engineer Jerry Burgess reckons his bike development skills exceed Micky D's. Remarkable for someone aged just 22.

'With Mick there was never much for us to do, because he'd win races by sheer mental and physical strength,' says Burgess. 'As long as the bike was about right, he could race it, he tended to put everything on himself. It's great with Valentino because he wants to work at making the bike better. I think it's because he came from 125s and 250s, where you have to get the most out of the machine to win. Mick came to 500s from Superbikes, which are less technically accurate.'

When Valentino quit Aprilia at the end of 1999 to graduate to 500s with Honda, the NSR was losing its dominance. Alex Criville, who won the '99 500 title

Possibly the most awesome and compact engine ever built – the NSR's tiny V4 motor delivers over 190hp. (James Wright)

Vale's input was vital in the creation of the 2002 NSR, the last in the line of a V4 two-stroke dynasty that started way back in 1984. (James Wright)

Honda **NSR500 2001**
Engine specifications

Type	liquid-cooled V4 two-stroke, reed-valve induction, with adjustable ignition, exhaust control etc
Bore & stroke	54 x 54.5mm
Displacement	499cc
Fuel system	four 36mm magnesium Keihin carbs
Claimed output	195hp at 12,500rpm
Gearbox	six-speed, cassette type

Chassis specifications

Frame type	dual beam aluminium
Tyres	Michelin
Wheels	17in front, 16.5in rear
Front brake	four-pot Brembo, twin 320mm carbon discs (dry), twin cast-iron discs (wet)
Rear-breake	two-pot Brembo, single 196mm disc
Front suspension	47mm upside down Showa, multi-adjustable
Rear suspension	Pro-Link with Showa shock, multi-adjustable
Wheelbase	1,400mm
Length	2,010mm
Race weight	131kg

after Doohan smacked himself up, had taken Honda down the wrong road on engine development. The Spaniard had asked HRC for more horsepower (a mistake that many racers make) and that's the last thing the NSR needed. With more power the NSR got slower, not faster, because it became more difficult to ride. It was Valentino who saved the day.

'Valentino was like a new brain for Honda, his mind was unpolluted and uncluttered by some of the NSR phobias the other guys may have had,' adds Burgess. 'He gave clear and honest comments that gave the engineers something to get their teeth into. Because he was new to the bike, he wanted to work on things that Mick and Alex had got used to because they'd always been that way. Also, Valentino rides different to Mick. He still has a bit of a 250 style, he doesn't hang off as far as Mick used to, and he ran the bike higher than Mick did, to get it steered.'

Honda pretty quickly realised that the young genius deserved a new NSR. 'The old bike had a lack of rear traction compared to the Yamaha and Suzuki, so Valentino would be spinning the rear rather than going forward,' Burgess continues. 'They built a new bike for

Making sense of the squiggly lines, Vale and Jerry Burgess examine NSR data. (Henk Keulemans)

the last few races of 2000, with the engine higher and further back for better acceleration traction.'

And traction, especially rear-end traction, is everything in big-bike racing, as rival Suzuki engineer Warren Willing explains: 'To get the best race time out of a 500 you have to compromise, you mustn't abuse the tyres any more than necessary. It's about understanding the dynamics and the interaction that's going on between rider and bike and remembering that all the forces on the motorcycle are driven through the tyres. All the horsepower in the world doesn't equate to any force if it's not hooked up. It's all in the tyres: how the suspension effects them, how the engine effects them, the rider, the track temperature and so on.'

HRC's decision to shift the NSR's centre of mass didn't only improve the bike out of turns. 'The higher engine position also threw more weight on to the front during braking, improving traction into turns,' Burgess explains. 'Then we just played around with suspension and linkages to fix the speed of weight transfer from rear to front.'

Finally, the shift in overall balance also helped fix the NSR's oldest problem – understeer. The bike had always been known for drifting wide through corners, and that's one reason for Doohan's famous hunched-over-the-front riding style; he was desperately trying to get more weight up front.

Valentino, Burgess and HRC also worked at improving the NSR's already very linear power delivery. Like Doohan before him, Valentino prioritised a user-friendly mid-range over peak horsepower because 500 riding is all about meting out the power, and you can't do that if the power curve isn't right. That's why his 2001 NSR was equipped with uber-trick magnesium Keihins, of which there were only two sets in existence. No other Honda rider was deemed worthy of them. Of course, even with that kind of help, 500 racing was always like riding the razor's edge for Valentino, and that's why he so loved his NSR. The new breed of GP four-strokes may be quicker but they don't give that same skating-on-the-edge-of-disaster feeling that racers crave. When a rider gets it right on a 500, he's climbed Mount Everest.

Chris Walker, who had a torrid crash-happy time with an NSR during 2001, puts it like this: 'If you go through a corner on a 500 and don't get it quite right and you think about it, you've missed the next turn! There's so much thinking, the trouble is that everything happens so fast. If you make a mistake, you're generally wearing it, whereas on a Superbike they give you some warning. On a 500, you miss a gear going into a corner and that's it, you've crashed. Do that on a Superbike and you'll probably be all right, you bang down the gears and find one, run wide and maybe touch the grass, but you get away with it. If you watch a 500 GP there's not many mistakes made because a mistake generally means a crash.'

Fast but fickle
Aprilia RSW250
1998/1999

Aprilia has enjoyed so much success over the past decade that it's easy to forget just how short a time the little Italian factory has been with us. The first Aprilia grand prix bike was built in 1985, a kind of backyard special using a Rotax 250 motor, and yet by the time Valentino won the 1999 250 crown the factory had won ten world titles and over 100 GPs in the 250 and 125 categories.

Like Soichiro Honda almost half a century before him, Aprilia founder Ivan Beggio is well into his racing, and it was Aprilia's track successes that quickly established the brand as a serious player in the Italian and then the world markets. Neither is there any doubt that the company's relationship with the two highest-profile Italian racers of recent years – Valentino and before him Max Biaggi – helped burn the marque into the public consciousness.

In turn, both Valentino and Biaggi have been lucky to have had Aprilia around. It is Italy's motorcycle industry that has helped foster so many Italian stars, and without Aprilia, their climb to the top of the sport would almost certainly have been much more difficult. Good machinery is vital in motorsport, without it even the best riders can fail to make the most of their talent, so it's not inconceivable that Valentino and Biaggi would never have made it without Aprilia around.

Valentino was also lucky that the Aprilia RSW250 was the most competitive 250 when he graduated to the class in 1998. In fact, '98 was the factory's best-ever year in GP racing, the RSW winning all but one of the season's 15 races. It hadn't always been so, for although Aprilia's 250s had always been fast, they'd also been fragile and fickle.

If Aprilia's RSW250 V-twin was fickle, it was also very, very fast. (Milagro)

Aprilia RSW250 1999	
Engine specifications	
Type	liquid-cooled, 90° V-twin two-stroke, disc-valve induction, with adjustable ignition, exhaust control
Bore & stroke	54 x 54.5mm
Displacement	249.6cc
Fuel system	two 42mm DellOrto carbs
Claimed output	over 96hp at 12,500rpm
Gearbox	six-speed, cassette type
Chassis specifications	
Frame type	dual beam aluminium
Tyres	Dunlop
Wheels	17in front and rear
Front brake	four-pot Brembo, twin 255/273mm carbon discs (dry), twin cast-iron discs (wet)
Rear-breake	two-pot Brembo, single 190mm disc
Front suspension	42mm upside down Ohlins, multi-adjustable
Rear suspension	carbon swingarm with Ohlins shock, multi-adjustable
Wheelbase	1,270mm
Length	1,970mm
Race weight	96kg

With his 250
crew in '98.
(Milagro)

Vale and his
RSW250's
gearbox. Better
stick to the
riding. (Milagro)

Aprilia won its first 250 GP in 1987, with Loris Reggiani on board, but it wasn't until '92 that the bike became consistently competitive against its Japanese rivals, Biaggi, Reggiani and Frankie Chili all scoring famous victories over main rivals Honda. It was another two years before race wins were turned into championship wins, Biaggi dominating the 1994, '95 and '96 campaigns before defecting to Honda.

The Aprilia's winning speed has always been attributed to one major factor – its intake system. While all the Japanese 250s – Honda's NSR, Yamaha's YZR and Suzuki's RGV – use reed-valve induction, the RSW uses disc-valve induction. Disc valves offer the opportunity for higher peak power output but with a trade-off in lower-rpm usability, while reeds do the opposite, delivering heaps of user-friendly mid-range but rather strangling the engine at peak revs.

In its earlier days the Aprilia probably suffered more than it gained from its uniqueness, for while the bike was a rocketship in a straight line, with a maniacally fast pick-up, it was slow out of the corners because riders struggled to cope with the vicious power delivery. But as electronics developed during the Nineties, that awkwardness was tamed, thanks to much-improved ignition systems and exhaust power-valves. GP racing's switch to unleaded fuel in '98 also calmed things down.

Nevertheless, the RSW's powerband was still crazily narrow – with the real business tucked between 12,000 and 13,000rpm – so Valentino didn't find the RSW the easiest of machines to master in '98. While he was immediately fast on the bike, it chucked him off at every opportunity in their first season together. He crashed out of no less than four races in '98.

'I'm still riding my 250 like it's a 125,' said Valentino midway through his debut 250 season. 'I am trying to learn something from my team-mates Harada and Capirossi but it doesn't work to change your own style too much, everyone has their own way of riding a motorcycle. I ride very different from Harada and Capirossi. If you watch Harada he's so smooth and makes it look easy, so you try to do the same, but it doesn't work. At Jerez, when I was racing with

Capirossi for the win, I tried to follow his lines, but that made me slower. Four laps from the end I went back to my own style, and I caught him a little.

'Harada is very clean while Capirossi brakes very, very hard all the way into the corner, then he goes very slow mid-corner, then he gets on the gas, hard! That's more like a 500 riding style, and I suppose he learned that from '95 and '96 when he was riding 500s. I don't brake so deep, I don't stop mid-corner and I'm a little more gentle on the gas – I have very much fear of the highside!' Even in their second year together, Valentino found the RSW a real handful in the wet, finishing a very uncharacteristic seventh and eighth in the two wet races of '99.

In fact, the Aprilia's bad behaviour can't wholly be blamed on its finicky engine configuration. It took years for factory engineers to get the bike's chassis fully sorted. Initially, the RSW's twin-beam aluminium frame – ostensibly the same as its rivals – was too stiff, giving riders a scary, edgy feel which failed to induce confidence through some corners and at some circuits. No wonder Valentino found the NSR500 so easy to get on with when he quit Aprilia at the end of '99.

Rossi's learner special
Aprilia RS125R
1995/1996/1997

Even the fastest 125 GP bikes aren't imposing machines, until you see a bunch of them involved in a scary mid-race encounter, their riders taking the kind of risks that would get them into serious trouble on a MotoGP bike. If MotoGP racing is a hi-tech confrontation between outrageously over-powerful surface-attack missiles, then 125 GP racing is good ol' fashioned hand-to-hand combat.

In 125s, it's not the bikes that are impressive, it's what the riders can do with them that's impressive. A 125 forgives where a 250 or MotoGP bike won't, so 125 racing is a great way for a rider to smooth off his roughest edges, before moving on to more demanding, more dangerous machines. In 125s throttle control is not very important, with less than 50hp available you can take big greedy handfuls and (probably) get away with it.

Unlike big-bike racing, throttle control isn't what

Aprilia RS125R 1997	
Engine specifications	
Type	liquid-cooled, single-cylinder two-stroke, disc-valve induction, with adjustable ignition, exhaust control
Bore & stroke	54 x 54.5mm
Displacement	124.8cc
Fuel system	39mm DellOrto carb
Claimed output	over 45hp at 12,700rpm
Gearbox	six-speed, cassette type
Chassis specifications	
Frame type	dual beam aluminium
Tyres	Dunlop
Wheels	17in front and rear
Front brake	four-pot Brembo, single carbon disc (dry), single cast-iron disc (wet)
Rear-brake	two-pot Brembo, single steel disc
Front suspension	35mm upside down Ohlins, multi-adjustable
Rear suspension	aluminum swingarm with Ohlins shock, multi-adjustable
Wheelbase	1,250mm
Length	1,970mm
Race weight	71kg

Puny but effective. Vale's '97 Aprilia 125 made less than 50hp. (Henk Keulemans)

really matters in 125s. What really matters is maintaining momentum, and that means super-fast corner entry and mid-corner speeds. That's why 125 riders are always bouncing off each other as they fight for the fast line. The bikes have so little power that you must never scrub off more speed through a turn than absolutely necessary. In fact, they have so little power that 125 riders believe it's worth bringing a little bit of foot power into the equation, frantically paddling away from the start of each race.

Valentino learned plenty from his Aprilia 125. He spent four years on different versions of the tiny single, initially with a Sandroni special in the '94 Italian championship, then in the '95 Euro and Italian series, then in GPs, winning his first World Championship success at Brno in August '96, then dominating the following season to wrap up his first world title.

The 125's engine internals are very similar to the 250's with almost identical porting arrangements, but with only half the 250's horsepower, so the 125 rolls over and dies if it slips out of its powerband. To keep the bike moving well, Valentino had to play hard and fast with the ultra-close ratio gearbox, trying to keep the tacho bouncing around in the 12 to 13,000rpm zone. That was agony in the old days, because the vibration caused havoc with a certain part of the male anatomy, but Aprilia generously added a countershaft balancer before Valentino came along.

Size is important in 125s, the smaller the better, which explains why Valentino's RSR tipped the scales at a puny 71kg, less than half the weight of his RCV four-stroke. Everything about the bike is puny, from the miniscule aluminium twin-beam chassis (again, a shrunken version of its big brother 250) to the skinny Dunlop slicks. The RSR is a learner GP bike, so it's got to be easy to throw around and easy to dominate. And there can be no doubt that the bike helped Rossi on the path to big-bike glory.

career
statistics

Minimoto mayhem
in the early
nineties. (Rossi
family archive)

1989   First go-kart race

1990   Regional go-kart champion; nine race wins

1991   5th – Italian junior Go-kart Championship
Wins first minimoto race

1992   1st – Regional Minimoto Championship

1993   3rd – 125 Italian Sport Production Championship –
Bike: Lusuardi Cagiva Mito

1994   1st – 125 Italian Sport Production Championship – Bike: Cagiva Mito
6th – 125 Italian Championship – Bike: Sandroni RS125R

1995   1st – 125 Italian Championship – Bike: Aprilia RS125R
3rd – 125 European Championship – Bike: Aprilia RS125R

'This time, don't
crash it!' Graziano
and Cagiva's
Claudio Lusuardi
offer some
heartfelt advice in
'93. (Rossi archive)

1996   125 World Championship – Bike: AGV Aprilia RS125R

Date	Event	Grid	Race
31.3	Malaysian GP, Shah Alam	13th	6th
7.4	Indonesian GP, Sentul	18th	11th
21.4	Japanese GP, Suzuka	10th	11th
12.5	Spanish GP, Jerez	7th	4th
26.5	Italian GP, Mugello	8th	4th
9.6	French GP, Paul Ricard	13th	DNF, crash/FL
29.6	Dutch GP, Assen	8th	DNF, crash
7.7	German GP, Nürburgring	4th	5th
21.7	British GP, Donington Park	9th	DNF, mech
4.8	Austrian GP, A1-Ring	3rd	3rd
18.8	Czech GP, Brno	pole	1st
1.9	City of Imola GP, Imola	2nd	5th/FL
15.9	Catalan GP, Catalunya	5th	DNF, crash
6.10	Rio GP, Jacarepagua	11th	DNF, crash
20.10	Australian GP, Eastern Creek	12th	14th

Overall championship position: 9th

Abbreviations:
DNF – did not finish;
FL – fastest lap;
mech – machine failure

His first ride with the GP guys, 'Fack, they were so fast!' (Gold & Goose)

1997 **125 World Championship** – Bike: Nastro Azzurro Aprilia RS125R

13.4	Malaysian GP, Shah Alam	pole	1st/FL
20.4	Japanese GP, Suzuka	7th	DNF, crash
4.5	Spanish GP, Jerez	6th	1st/FL
18.5	Italian GP, Mugello	3rd	1st
1.6	Austrian GP, A1-Ring	2nd	2nd/FL
8.6	French GP, Paul Ricard	3rd	1st
28.6	Dutch GP, Assen	pole	1st
6.7	City of Imola	pole	1st/FL
20.7	German GP, Nürburgring	pole	1st
3.8	Rio GP, Jacarepagua	2nd	1st/FL
17.8	British GP, Donington Park	4th	1st/FL
31.8	Czech GP, Brno	3rd	3rd
14.9	Catalan GP, Catalunya	4th	1st
28.9	Indonesian GP	4th	1st/FL
5.10	Australian GP, Phillip Island	3rd	6th

Overall championship position: 1st

Valentino didn't have to run away from home to join the two-wheel GP circus. (Milagro)

1998 **250 World Championship** – Bike: Nastro Azzurro Aprilia RSW250

5.4	Japanese GP, Suzuka	7th	DNF, mech
19.4	Malaysian GP, Johor	2nd	DNF, crash/FL
3.5	Spanish GP, Jerez	3rd	2nd
17.5	Italian GP, Mugello	4th	2nd
31.5	French GP, Paul Ricard	3rd	2nd
14.6	Madrid GP, Jarama	4th	DNF, crash
27.6	Dutch GP, Assen	3rd	1st
5.7	British GP, Donington Park	2nd	DNF, crash
19.7	German GP, Sachsenring	4th	3rd
23.8	Czech GP, Brno	2nd	DNF, crash
6.9	City of Imola GP, Imola	5th	1st
20.9	Catalan GP, Catalunya	2nd	1st/FL
4.10	Australian GP, Phillip Island	2nd	1st
25.10	Argentine GP, Buenos Aires	3rd	1st/FL

Overall championship position: 2nd

His mum wanted him to be a footballer. Vale still plays games for charity. (Milagro)

1999 **250 World Championship** – Bike: Nastro Azzurro Aprilia RSW250

18.4	Malaysian GP, Sepang	pole	5th
25.4	Japanese GP, Motegi	11th	7th
9.5	Spanish GP, Jerez	3rd	1st
23.5	French GP, Paul Ricard	pole	DNF, mech/FL
6.6	Italian GP, Mugello	6th	1st/FL
20.6	Catalan GP, Catalunya	2nd	1st/FL
27.6	Dutch GP, Assen	pole	2nd/FL
4.7	British GP, Donington Park	3rd	1st
18.7	German GP, Sachsenring	pole	1st
22.8	Czech GP, Brno	3rd	1st/FL
5.9	City of Imola GP, Imola	3rd	2nd
19.9	Valencia GP, Valencia	4th	8th
3.10	Australian GP, Phillip Island	7th	1st/FL
10.10	South African GP, Welkom	6th	1st/FL
24.10	Rio GP, Jacarepagua	2nd	1st/FL
31.10	Argentine GP, Buenos Aires	pole	3rd

Overall championship position: 1st

With former girlfriend Eliane Ferni, Phillip Island '99. (Milagro)

The wolf man meets the media at Suzuka 2002. (Gold & Goose)

Japanese GP practice and about to jump off, twice. (Gold & Goose)

2000 **500 World Championship** – Bike: Nastro Azzurro Honda NSR500

19.3	South African GP, Welkom	5th	DNF, crash/FL
2.4	Malaysian GP, Sepang	7th	DNF, crash
9.4	Japanese GP, Suzuka	13th	11th
30.4	Spanish GP, Jerez	2nd	3rd
14.5	French GP, Le Mans	10th	3rd/FL
28.5	Italian GP, Mugello	3rd	DNF/crash
11.6	Catalan GP, Catalunya	9th	3rd
24.6	Dutch GP, Assen	6th	6th
9.7	British GP, Donington Park	4th	1st
23.7	German GP, Sachsenring	6th	2nd
20.8	Czech GP, Brno	5th	2nd
3.9	Portuguese GP, Estoril	12th	3rd/FL
17.9	Valencia GP, Valencia	5th	DNF, crash
7.10	Rio GP, Jacarepagua	4th	1st/FL
15.10	Pacific GP, Motegi	5th	2nd/FL
29.10	Australian GP, Phillip Island	8th	3rd

Overall championship position: 2nd

2001 **500 World Championship** – Bike: Nastro Azzurro Honda NSR500

8.4	Japanese GP, Suzuka	7th	1st
22.4	South African GP, Welkom	pole	1st/FL
6.5	Spanish GP, Jerez	pole	1st/FL
20.5	French GP, Le Mans	3rd	3rd
3.6	Italian GP, Mugello	pole	DNF, crash/FL
17.6	Catalan GP, Catalunya	pole	1st/FL
30.6	Dutch GP, Assen	3rd	2nd/FL
8.7	British GP, Donington Park	11th	1st/FL
22.7	German GP, Sachsenring	11th	7th
26.8	Czech GP, Brno	2nd	1st/FL
9.9	Portuguese GP, Estoril	3rd	1st
23.9	Valencia GP, Valencia	2nd	11th
7.10	Pacific GP, Motegi	4th	1st/FL
14.10	Australian GP, Phillip Island	2nd	1st
21.10	Malaysian GP, Sepang	2nd	1st/FL
3.11	Rio GP, Jacarepagua	5th	1st/FL

Overall championship position: 1st

2002 **MotoGP World Championship** – Bike: Repsol Honda RCV211V

7.4	Japanese GP, Suzuka	pole	1st
21.4	South African GP, Welkom	pole	2nd
5.5	Spanish GP, Jerez	pole	1st
19.5	French GP, Le Mans	pole	1st

index